how to Love Your Flute

A Guide to

Flutes and

Flute Playing

by Mark Shepard

Illustrated by Anne Subercaseaux

PANJANDRUM BOOKS

BERKELEY AND LOS ANGELES

Library of Congress Cataloging in Publication Data

Shepard, Mark, 1950–
   How to love your flute.

   Includes bibliography.
   1. Flute.   I. Title.
ML935.S5   788'.51   79–9147
ISBN 0-915572-36-2

Design, copyediting, production by Zipporah W. Collins

Panjandrum Books, 11321 Iowa Avenue, Suite 8, Los Angeles, California 90025

Manufactured in the United States of America

May we
be made
ever more perfect
instruments.

Photo and Illustration Credits

All photos in part I of current-day folk flute players reprinted courtesy of Alexander Buchner.

All historical photos in part I reprinted courtesy of the Library of Congress.

Photos of modern flutes and modern flute manufacture in parts I and II reprinted courtesy of W. T. Armstrong Co.

All photos in part III by Russell Redmond, as well as figure 117 (appearing after part V), and the photo of the author.

Photo of shakuhachi in part V reprinted courtesy of Monty H. Levenson. Flute by Monty H. Levenson, P.O. Box 294, Willits, California 95490.

All other photos of flutes in part V by Mark Shepard and Lillian Gurenson. Bamboo transverse flute by Mark Shepard. Ceramic transverse flute by Reliable Brothers, California. Kena by Gabor, P.O. Box 55, Hayfork, California 96041. Panpipes by Patrick Olwell, Route 1, Box 76A, Roseland, Virginia 22967.

All drawings, except those in part I, by Anne Subercaseaux.

In part I, the illustration of Renaissance flutes (figure 10) comes from *Musica instrumentalis deudsch*, Martin Agricola (1545); the Baroque flute (figure 12) from *Principes de la Flute Traversiere*, Jacques Hotteterre (1707); the eight-key flute (figure 13) from Rockstro's *Treatise on the Flute* (1890).

Contents

Part III   Flute Technique

Appendix

Preface

Mark Shepard has come up with the most unique flute manual I have ever seen. It is direct, complete, informative on every aspect, and—most important—comes from the standpoint of pure love and respect for the instrument. Some good down-home philosophy is included too—on practicing and discipline ("Should you have a fixed practice period every day? This depends on how you personally learn best."); on reading versus playing by ear ("This is strictly a matter of personal preference, depending on how you feel you would like to play. There's no reason you can't do both, if you like").

He gives some wonderful pointers on care and maintenance. Imagine—after 25 years I find out I shouldn't be leaving my cleaning swab inside the flute case when I pack my flute away; and that Q-tips shouldn't be used to clean out the embouchure hole. How embarrassing!

Today the flute is enjoying unprecedented popularity. People are buying and playing flutes for the pure, simple pleasure of it, and not necessarily with the goal of becoming professional musicians. (The great therapeutic value of flute playing is alone reason enough to go out and get a flute immediately!) Standard flute method books are for the most part stiff, pedantic, boring—and obsolete, in light of this new trend of flutists geared to pop and jazz music and simple, free, solo improvisation. Mark Shepard's book serves as a model for our times, and it is an inspiration for those who want to get more out of life through the joys of flute playing.

Paul Horn

Acknowledgments

Thanks to Bruce Kanne and Dale Robertson, who introduced me to the flute; to my father, Bruce Gurenson, for some crucial financial assistance; to Gale Kramvik, John Neptune, Monty H. Levenson, Norman P. Maloney (of Rudall, Carte), and others, for helpful criticism of the manuscript, with extra thanks to Gale for proofreading the galleys; to Sara Wright, Kathy Dinaburg, and Paul Sutherland, who gave invaluable suggestions leading to publication; to Hank Maiden, my Quaker agent; to Dennis Koran, my editor, and the others at Panjandrum; to Russell Redmond, for his generous photo work; to Anne Subercaseaux, for her diligence, patience, and skill in preparing the illustrations; and to Paul Horn, for his great generosity in providing a preface for this book. Special thanks to my mother, Lillian Gurenson, whose selfless support made the writing of this book possible.

Above all, thanks to God, to whom all glory is due.

how to
Love
Your
Flute

Introductions

My Love Affair with the Flute

For some time now I have been involved in an intense love affair with the flute.

I first became attracted to the instrument because a good friend of mine happened to be an excellent flutist. We played together often (I on conga drums), and as time went on I felt more and more drawn to the sound of the flute. But the idea of trying myself to play the flute—such a difficult, mysterious instrument—was quite beyond me.

The breakthrough came when another friend of mine, a bamboo flute maker, forced me to sit down with one of his flutes and get a sound out of it. It took several minutes, but I finally managed to force out a tone—much to my amazement. After that, nothing could stop me. A good portion of each day I would be lost in playing my bamboo flute, and I often carried it around with me to play in spare moments. As my needs developed, I switched to a modern flute, which gradually became my main instrument.

During this time I discovered some important things about the flute. One was how beautiful the sound of it really is. I must admit, I believe there is no other instrument that can surpass it in loveliness. The extreme simplicity and purity of the flute tone sets it in a class by itself.

I was also very pleased to discover what flute playing did for me personally. I found that I was always coming away from the flute a little more "together" than I had been. No matter how upset, tense, or nervous I was when I picked up the flute, I would become calm and peaceful after a little playing. I even found that, when I was ill, playing made me feel physically better.

To what do I attribute these healing properties of the flute? In part they are probably related to the full breathing required for flute playing. Cleaning out the lungs and supplying adequate air to the body have to produce some good effect. But I also sincerely believe that the flute vibrations themselves are health-giving on the physical, psychological, and spiritual levels.

Probably the most important element, though, is the concentration required to learn to play. You forget all your troubles, because there's no extra room in your mind to hold them! Your thought becomes completely focused, and this can't help but be restful. In essence, learning to play the flute is a disguised form of meditation.

These are my own ideas about why flute playing did such good things for me, but whatever the reasons the results were apparent. I couldn't help noticing what it was doing for other people also. After the first few months of my playing, people hearing the flute would tend to "float away" on its sound. It would carry them off, and when they returned, they would seem to be happier, more at peace with themselves. This was not due to any great technical ability on my part. I simply had developed very early the knack of letting the flute speak as it wished.

So I found that flute playing was improving the quality of my own life and the lives of the people around me. It occurred to me that such a force for good should be spread around, made available to more people. I began to want to share the flute with others. It was out of that desire that this book was conceived and written.

About This Book

The main purpose of this book is to serve as a comprehensive guide for those starting out on the flute. In this respect, it can be used as a tool for self-teaching or as a supplement to lessons. More advanced players may find themselves interested in particular sections—on flutes around the world, repairs, etc.—that contain some material not previously found in books on the flute.

In an attempt to meet the needs of a wide range of flutists, sections have been included both on playing by ear and on reading music. These should be helpful not only to the beginner but also to the advanced player who is currently limited to one type of playing and would like to explore the other.

Finally, a special section has been included on the selection, care, and playing of modern folk flutes.

The five main parts of the book are fairly independent, so that readers can jump from one to another without great difficulty. Within each part, however, the material follows a progression and is best read in order. It is especially recommended that beginners using part III, "Flute Technique," follow the order of the chapters.

Common Questions from Beginners

If you are a beginner on the flute, you may have certain questions about how best to go about learning the instrument. For instance, should you take lessons or teach yourself instead?

There are advantages to both ways. You may be a person who will benefit more from personal instruction than from reading a book such as this, for instance. Or you may be the type of person who needs the deadlines of a scheduled lesson to get you to practice. If you are serious about performing classical music, you will want to become absorbed in a tradition that seems to be imparted best in a teacher/student relationship.

There are also advantages to teaching yourself. Money and/or schedule constraints could be factors. You might prefer (as I do) the freedom of organizing and pacing your own learning process. Or you might even have trouble finding a teacher with whom you work well, or who can teach you the kind of flute playing you want to learn.

Whichever way you decide to go, don't let anyone tell you that you *can't* learn flute without lessons. Many flutists have taught and are teaching themselves and have become quite good without formal training of any kind. (I speak from experience: I have never had a formal flute lesson, and yet I have played professionally for several years.)

If you decide to take lessons, it's essential that the teacher you choose have a good rapport with you, be able to convey his/her knowledge in an exciting, involving way, and be able to teach you the kind of playing that *you* want to do. Finding the right teacher can mean a vital, enriching learning experience. Taking lessons from the wrong teacher can frustrate your energy, and even destroy your love of the instrument.

Should you have a fixed practice period every day? This depends on how you personally learn best. You may find that the discipline of a fixed practice period helps you focus your energy, and produces a steadier progression in your learning. Or you may find you work best by picking up the flute when you feel moved to and playing it only as long as the impulse lasts. Or you may hit on some balance between these two extremes.

Many times students are told that they must practice every day, or they will "lose what they have." This may be true for advanced players, but it doesn't seem to be the case for beginners. Many musicians (myself included) can tell of having shoved aside their instruments for weeks at a time, only to discover when they picked them up again that their playing had actually improved!

Should you do exercises as a regular part of

your practicing? Again, it depends on how you learn best. Exercises can definitely be helpful in building your technique. On the other hand, it isn't worth while to spend a great deal of time "building your technique" if it destroys your love of playing. You will have to explore this for yourself. (Possible exercises are suggested in various parts of the book, especially in chapter 9.)

Should you learn to read music or play by ear instead? This is strictly a matter of personal preference, depending on how you feel you would like to play. There's no reason you can't do both, if you like! Of course, playing classical music will require you to read; improvising popular music or jazz means playing by ear.

Contrary to popular myth, it is not necessary to learn to read music before you can play by ear. (As Pete Seeger says, "Would you teach a baby to read before it could talk?") If anything, learning to read music first makes playing by ear more difficult, since you then have to overcome your dependence on the printed page. Another destructive myth is that only those people who are "musical" can play by ear. Anyone can! (See chapter 15, "Playing by Ear.")

Are there any other resources you should use to help you learn the flute? Yes, plenty of them. Listen to records. Go to flute performances. Stop flute players on the street. Ask questions. Play different flutes. Soak up everything that you hear or read, test it, see if it works for you. The whole world is your teacher. All you have to do is coax it a little.

How to Love Your Flute

What exactly do I mean by "how to love your flute"?

There seem to be two ways of approaching the flute. One is in the spirit of domination: the learner attempts to "conquer" the flute, to force from it the secrets of its operation, to subordinate it to his or her own musical wishes.

It is an attitude of "overcoming." This is not how to love your flute!

Loving your flute means being aware that you and the instrument are coproducers of the music, partners in the creation of sound. It means becoming aware of the instrument's requirements, its musical preferences, its reactions to your own wishes. If you attempt to subjugate the instrument, it will fight you at every step; if you respect and work with it, you will find it responding willingly and demonstratively. As this relationship deepens, you and the flute can begin to grow together and gradually become, in effect, one instrument.

A major aim of this book is to help you develop a sensitivity toward the flute and its interrelationships with you, the player. When you approach the flute in a spirit of love, the instrument itself will also teach you. If you are open to what it has to say, it will itself let you know how it should be played. And the instrument is always the best teacher.

In this special relationship, the lessons it offers may go beyond mere flute playing. The instrument can also teach you lessons about learning, about life, about love—because the same laws that govern the playing of a flute also govern the workings of the world around you and the world within you. In this way the flute can become a focal point for the growth of understanding, a pathway to wisdom. Hermann Hesse, in his book *Siddhartha,* tells us that a person can eventually come to understand the entire universe by starting from any point within it—a butterfly, a rock, a river. The flute is such a point of departure.

There is truly much to be gained from a relationship with the flute—the enjoyment of its sound, the joy of creating music, the peace of a focused outpouring of the spirit, the insights that come with an openness to lessons taught. May all these and more be yours, as you grow in the love of your flute.

Part I

Flute Lore

1
The World Family of Flutes

The instrument we know as "the" flute is really only one important member of a very large world family of flutes. In this chapter we'll discuss some of the other members of this family.

But first we should describe what a "flute" is. Classifiers of musical instruments define a flute as any instrument in which the sound is produced by the movement of the player's breath against an edge. In side-blown flutes, such as our modern instrument, this edge is the one opposite the mouth hole. In end-blown flutes, such as the *nay* and the *shakuhachi*, the edge is the open end of the tube—whether sharpened, cut obliquely, notched, or left plain. There is also a large group of instruments called *block flutes*, which direct the air against an edge by use of a

mouthpiece or channeling arrangement. Recorders and penny whistles are common instruments in this group.

Now let's take a brief tour of the world of flutes. But we can hit only a few highlights. The full variety of flutes and their appearances around the world would take an entire book to describe—if they could be covered at all!

South America

Let's begin in what is probably the center of flute activity in the world—the Andes Mountains of South America. In the musical gatherings of the highland Indians, flutes of all kinds are the undisputed lead instruments.

Chief among these is the *kena*, an end-blown flute usually made from bamboo. This ancient flute is older than the Incas—one bamboo kena found preserved in sand in Peru is estimated to be about 10,000 years old! The kena was originally a pentatonic (five-note) flute, but, after coming under the influence of Spanish music, it was adapted to the Western scale. It is played with a throat vibrato that gives it a fluttering, birdlike quality.

Panpipes are another common type of Andean flute. These are made of a series of bamboo or reed tubes of different lengths, without finger holes, closed at the bottom end, and bound together in a row (see figure 1 at the beginning of this chapter). They are blown exactly as a pop bottle would be. Each tube gives one note only, so in order to play a tune the flutist has to move around to another tube pretty fast! Often this is made easier by tying together two rows of pipes,

Figure 1

containing alternate notes. The two rows are sometimes untied and played by two people. Each player then fills in the notes left out by the other. Some very energetic duets are played this way.

This duet of panpipes is also done in large groups. In festivals in some parts of the Andes, the panpipers will split into two groups—each group playing one "row" of pipes—and play at each other across a field. In other types of large-group playing, many different sizes of panpipes are used, some of the larger tubes ranging up to four feet in length. These panpipe orchestras can contain as many as forty instruments.

Ocarinas are also popular in this area. These are globular block flutes—not tubes at all—usually made of clay. On an ocarina, it doesn't matter where the holes are placed, or in what order the player fingers them—the more holes uncovered, the higher the note will be. Ocarinas are often made in the shapes of birds, animals, or humans and are colored brightly.

North America

North America is one of the chief strongholds of the modern flute, but the Indians

of this continent were also among the world's most extensive developers of the block flute (see figure 2). Their flutes are made of wood, bird bones, and shale. In the Central Woodlands and Great Plains areas, these flutes were traditionally used by young Indian men for serenading, to signal their affections to their lady loves. They also often were used in fertility rites and dances. Flutes are important symbols in Hopi rituals.

A whole new generation of folk flutes is springing up now in this area of the world. But we'll save that discussion for later (see chapter 17).

Africa

A great variety of flutes can be found in Africa, from simple one-note whistles to well-tuned end-blown flutes (see figure 3). Flute bands of various kinds are common. In one type of band in southern Africa, each player

Figure 2

Figure 3

holds a long pipe that produces one note. The player sounds that note at the appropriate place in the melody. The same pipe, however, is sometimes used by an individual player, who gets a variety of notes by altering the breath and by opening and closing the end of the tube with the hands.

In Africa, the flute is often believed to have supernatural powers. Its sound is used as an aid in various rituals, such as communicating with spirits, bringing rain, stopping storms, curing illnesses, and protecting from various dangers. Nose-flutes—flutes blown with the nose—are used by Africans and are considered especially potent, since breath from the nostrils is believed to contain the soul.

The Middle East

The Arabic countries are the home of the *nay*, a flute whose close relatives can be found throughout Africa and in Eastern Europe. The nay is a long, thin tube of cane or bamboo, with finger holes and a plain open end as a mouth hole. It is slanted toward the side of the player, and for this reason it is called a *diagonal* flute. To blow it, one edge of the open end is placed against the side of the mouth, while the lips, puckered as if to whistle or to sound the syllable "oo," point directly at the opposite edge. Because of the finger stretch required on this flute, the middle joint of each finger, rather than the fingertip, is used to cover the holes.

The thinness of the tube in relation to its length creates a wispy, ethereal tone that is quite appealing. It also makes the first octave practically impossible to play, so the normal playing scale on these flutes is considered to begin with the second octave. The nay is currently produced in lengths corresponding to all keys of the chromatic scale, and in seven different tunings to accommodate the large number of Arabic scales.

The earliest pictures of the nay in Egypt date from 6,000 years ago, and the instrument is often found in Egyptian tombs. An ancient legend attributed its origin to the water god, Osiris. The nay is the principal instrument of the Sufis and is used in their dervish dances.

Eastern Europe

A close relative of the nay is the *kaval,* a popular flute in Eastern Europe and Turkey (see figure 4). The kaval is made of wood,

Figure 4

often in sections. The top rim is beveled to create a sharper edge, making it slightly easier to play. The flutist sometimes hums a constant "drone" note as an accompaniment to the sound of the instrument.

The flute has been called "the universal pastoral pipe of the shepherd," and this claim is certainly borne out in Eastern Europe. The music of shepherds is an important part of much of the local culture, and the *shepherd's pipe,* a block flute with six holes, is one of their major instruments. Many other types of flutes are also used, including a double block flute, in which the second pipe can be used either to play a harmony or as a drone.

Beautiful carved wood panpipes are produced and played in Eastern Europe. Of course, Greece

Figure 5

is the source of the legend that gives the panpipes their name—by attributing their invention to the god Pan.

Western Europe

In Western Europe we find two basic types of flutes—block flutes and side-blown flutes. Common block flutes include the *recorder* and the *penny* or *tin whistle*. A three-holed whistle flute is also found in many of these countries, called by different names—*galoubet* in France, *fluviol* in Spain. It is played one-handed, while the other hand plays a drum, and it commonly accompanies folk dancing. By using harmonics, two octaves or more of a diatonic scale can be played. (These terms are discussed in the appendix and in chapter 13.)

It is in Western Europe that the side-blown flute underwent its most sophisticated development—as might be expected, considering the technological orientation of this part of the world. Eventually this evolution produced what we know as the modern flute. The story of that development is told in chapter 2.

India

Several types of flutes are mentioned in the Hindu holy books, the Vedas. The great god Krishna is said to have played the flute during his youth as a cowherd (as Indian shepherd boys still do today), and Indra played the flute when several gods came together to form a celestial band.

The side-blown flute first became popular in India about 2,000 years ago, and from that time on it has been by far the most important flute. The classical Indian side-blown flute is made from one joint of bamboo—Indian bamboo being very long-jointed, straight, regular, and thin-walled. There are normally six finger holes, which are covered (as on the nay and the kaval) with the middle joint of the fingers. An extra hole

Figure 6

is often placed at the end for the little finger, enabling the flutist to play one note lower in the first octave (much as on a modern flute's foot joint).

The main scale of these flutes is identical to the Western major scale. However, the Indians produce it differently. The note sounded with the first three holes closed is regarded as the first note of the scale, and the fourth note is played by half-holing the first hole. If the flute were played with the lowest note as the first note and no half-holing, a regular Western major scale would be heard.*

Many scales are used in Indian music, and to play them the Indian flutist must make extensive use of half-holing. (For an explanation of half-holing, see chapter 19.) Indian music also requires various shakes, slides, slurs, and other devices of great subtlety and delicate nuance, created by finger and breath techniques. These techniques cannot be used on the mechanized modern flute, since they require direct contact by the fingers with the holes. The modern flute, then, is a vastly inferior instrument for producing Indian stylistic effects. Indians also much prefer bamboo to metal for tonal quality.

China

The Chinese use a variety of flutes, including panpipes and both end-blown and side-blown flutes. The principal flute used today is the *ti,* a bamboo side-blown flute with six finger holes, usually lacquered, and bound with silk thread. It has an extra hole, above the first finger hole, that is covered with thin bamboo membrane or rice paper, to give a buzzing sound—like a kazoo—in addition to the flute tone. Two extra holes are made at the end of the flute, and a thread with beads and feathers on it is tied through them, for decoration and for hanging up the flute.

An ancient Chinese flute called the *tsche* was stopped at both ends, with the mouth hole in the center and the finger holes going off to the sides.

---

*This description of the flute's construction and scale applies to northern India, where most Indian music that Westerners hear originates. Southern India differs somewhat in this, as in many other respects.

Figure 7

Similar flutes can still be found in western Russia and in parts of Africa.

Oceania

Panpipes are found throughout the islands of the South Pacific and Australia. Melanesia (the set of islands northeast of Australia) shares with the Andes a reputation as one of the great panpiping regions of the world. Nose-flutes are also common.

In New Guinea, it is believed that spirits live in flutes. The instruments are housed in special shrines and worshiped before being brought out to be played in rites and ceremonies. Flutes are often used in fertility rites.

Japan

The traditional flutes of Japan, like many other aspects of Japanese culture, are adaptations of instruments introduced from China. The side-blown bamboo flute—called the *fue* by the Japanese, and now the most common type of traditional flute—first came to Japan this way. Since its introduction, it has been developed into a number of distinct forms, many of them identified with particular types of music—court music, theater music, festival music, etc.

Figure 8

Figure 9

different group of pieces as its basic repertoire. The schools are associations of individual teachers, generally working in their own homes or studios, passing on their traditions in a direct aural form to their students.

Another Japanese flute—the *shakuhachi*—is rapidly gaining prestige throughout the Western world.* It is an end-blown flute fashioned from the thick-walled root end of the bamboo pole, including a portion of the root ball itself. Its five finger holes give a pentatonic scale, but the entire chromatic scale in three octaves can be produced by half-holing, cross-fingering, and making lip adjustments (see chapter 19). The name *shakuhachi* means simply "one foot, eight (Japanese) inches," the length of the standard instrument. Shakuhachis are also made in both smaller and larger sizes, however.

In the hands of a master, the shakuhachi can produce sounds that amaze Western ears and that would be impossible to duplicate on the Western flute. Several different "schools" of shakuhachi playing exist in Japan, each one employing a slightly different style and using a

The construction of a good shakuhachi is a fine art. Bamboo pieces are cut only from thicker-walled poles of a particular species of Japanese bamboo. The piece is heated over a fire, to remove some of the resin, and then set aside to season for six months to two years or longer. If necessary, the piece is then heated again and bent into proper shape.

The bamboo is then generally cut into two sections, which are joined by a socket-and-tenon arrangement. The inside is rasped and filed to

---

*The shakuhachi first became widely known in the United States through a letter written by Monty H. Levenson, a flute maker from Willits, California, that was printed in the *Last Whole Earth Catalog* (1971).

develop an even taper that narrows toward the bottom, following approximately the natural bore of the bamboo. A critical cut made obliquely at the top of the flute creates a blowing edge, which is then inlaid with water buffalo horn, ivory, or (recently) plastic. Finger holes are drilled into the piece, using exact mathematical relationships. The inside is then coated with plaster, and painstakingly worked to precise measurements, using a series of gauges. Finally, a red or black lacquer that dries to a glossy finish is applied to the inside.*

The exact origin of the shakuhachi is uncertain, though it almost certainly had its roots in earlier Chinese flutes. It has existed in its

*This description applies to construction of shakuhachis in the Kinko and Tozan schools. Meian shakuhachis are made more simply. In addition, "student" models are now being manufactured from wood and plastic.

present form at least since the Edo period (1615–1868 A.D.) and possibly much earlier. The first shakuhachi musicians were Zen Buddhist monks, for whom playing the flute was a religious practice as well as a way of soliciting alms. From these beginnings, the shakuhachi gradually spread to other segments of the population.

Just as the Japanese formerly derived much from the Chinese, over the last century they have adopted many elements of Western culture, including classical and pop music forms. Western instruments—the modern flute among them—have become dominant in the urban centers, while traditional Japanese classical instruments have suffered a period of relative obscurity. Recently, however, the shakuhachi has experienced something of a revival. As the West is discovering this beautiful flute, the Japanese are *re*discovering it.

2
The Story
of the Western Flute

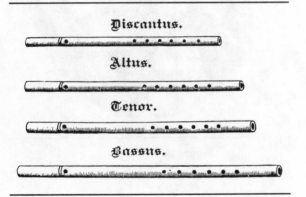

Western Europe was the birthplace of the modern flute. The side-blown flute first entered Europe as a popular instrument from Asia and spread westward over the continent in the late Middle Ages. The flute found throughout Europe around 1500 A.D. was not

Discantus.

Altus.

Tenor.

Bassus.

Figure 10

much different from its Oriental counterparts—a cylindrical tube made from wood, with six finger holes.

The Baroque Flute

The first major development away from this simple form came from France toward the end of the 1600s, probably as the result of work done by classical musicians and instrument makers in the court of Louis XIV. The flute they devised—which we now call the *Baroque flute*—had several revolutionary

Figure 11

features: First, to make it easier for the instrument maker to work on the bore (the hollowed out inside of the flute), the instrument was divided into three sections—the head, body, and foot joints we still have today. Secondly, the bore of the body joint was changed from cylindrical (constant diameter throughout) to conical (tapering to a narrower diameter at the bottom). This resulted in major improvements in the tuning between the octaves, and in the range of the flute.

The musicians and composers of this period preferred a flute tone that was "small," "pure," and "sweet," and this was achieved on the new flute both by the new bore and by the use of smaller finger holes. Finally, an extra hole was added on the foot joint, operated by a "closed" key—a key that covered the hole when at rest and lifted to open the hole when pressed (see figure 12). (A similar key can be found today on the alto recorder.)

Figure 12

This conical-bore flute became the basic form of the flute for the next century and a half, though its details underwent much development. For instance, more holes and keys (closed keys, except on the foot joint) were gradually added to make sharps and flats easier to play. By the end of the 1700s, flutes with eight keys were common (see figure 13).

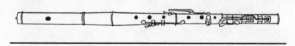

Figure 13

Experimentation on the flute continued and increased in the 1800s. The most successful of the experimenters was a German named Theobald Boehm, the inventor of the modern flute.

The Boehm Flute

During his life, Boehm was a jeweler and goldsmith, an improver of the modern piano, a steel technologist, a master flutist, and a flute maker. Dissatisfied with the

Figure 14
Theobald Boehm

flute of his time, Boehm wanted to develop an instrument that would have better tuning, a more even tone, and—most important of all—a loud, powerful sound. Over the years, interspersed with his other activities, Boehm developed a series of flute models that came increasingly close to his goals. Finally, in 1847—after a two-year period of acoustical study and experimentation—Boehm introduced a flute that is very nearly what we play today, a flute still technically known as the *Boehm flute*.

The features of Boehm's flute were radically

different from those of previous Western flutes. Boehm returned to the cylindrical bore of the pre-Baroque flute, but tapered the head joint slightly at the top. (The narrowing is visible on the modern flute.) The new taper retained the advantages of the previous conical bore, while improving the high and low notes. The holes were much enlarged and their positions changed accordingly, giving much better tuning, more volume, and a fuller tone. This rearrangement was made possible by a completely new key mechanism, based on open keys (ones that close when pushed down),* devices linking keys together, and the use of pads, rather than direct finger contact, to close all holes. This was also the first successful flute model in the modern West to be made of metal, though wooden Boehm flutes also continued to be made.

The Boehm flute is one of the finest examples of engineering in the history of musical instrument design, if not in the history of design itself. For the playing of Western music, it is technically far superior to the flutes that preceded it, yet it retains a simplicity of construction and technique—an elegance—that keeps it accessible. Perhaps no more total and successful transformation of an instrument has ever been accomplished by any one person before or since.

Since Boehm

Boehm's flute was not immediately hailed as the ultimate form of the instrument, however. On the contrary, its appearance sparked the development of a large number of different flute models—many of them grafts of the conical-bore flute to Boehm's, others concentrating on improving the conical-bore flute. Boehm's flute had to compete with all these new models, plus the models that had preceded it.

Boehm's own flute underwent some further modifications—not all of them improvements.

*Open keys should not be confused with open-holed keys, which are key covers that have an opening in them. Open keys refer to the manner of the key's functioning. Boehm did not use open-holed keys.

The most important of these changes came from France, in attempts to overcome resistance to the new instrument. The French partially reincorporated two features of the old flutes: holes were put in the centers of some keys (giving open-holed keys), and the G key was placed in line with the others. These changes created the French model flute of today. Another carryover modification was the closed G-sharp key, bitterly fought by Boehm as an acoustic compromise, but now used almost exclusively (except in Eastern Europe).

Many flutists actively opposed Boehm's flute. This was partly due to resistance to having to learn a whole new fingering system, but in many cases it was also because they did not like the sound of the instrument. They preferred the pure and sweet tone of the old flute to the openness and power of the new. For this very reason, the Boehm flute is still not widely accepted in some parts of Western Europe. Irish folk musicians still prefer the sound of the conical-bore, eight-keyed flute, which they call the concert flute. In Germany, Boehm's homeland, resistance to the new sound was the strongest. Nonprofessional players there often still use conical-bore flutes, some models showing very elaborate development of keywork and bore since the time of Boehm (see figure 15).

Figure 15

All in all, though, the Boehm flute has definitely advanced to first place among Western flutes. This was probably not because flutists liked its sound or recognized its technical superiority but rather because the classical orchestral playing of the time demanded the greater volume and projection that the new instrument could provide. As professional flutists shifted over to the new flute, they taught it to their pupils, who in turn taught it to theirs, until the Boehm flute achieved its present status. Several of Boehm's own pupils settled in North America, where a similar process occurred.

The growing influence of Western culture has now spread the Boehm flute to nearly all parts of the globe. However—since Western culture is mainly "city" culture—its use in non-Western countries is generally limited to urban areas.

Materials and Manufacture

Preferred materials have shifted over the years. Though wooden Boehm flutes are still fairly common in much of Europe, metal is now definitely the world favorite. In America and Japan, the wooden flute is almost unknown.

Modern metal flutes are made from seamless tubing, drawn by machine from metal discs. The tapered head joint is formed by pounding on a mandrel (a steel rod bearing the required shape). Soldering is used to attach the connecting tenons, beadings (ridges on the tube), mouthpiece tube, lip plate, and ribs and posts that hold the keywork. (See figure 16.)

The raised walls at the holes were also formerly soldered on, but they are now almost always drawn from the body of the flute itself. This is done by cutting a small hole in the tube, positioning a plug beneath it, then forcing the plug out through the hole. The walls raised in the process are then rolled over at the top to present a smooth surface to the pad (see figure 17).

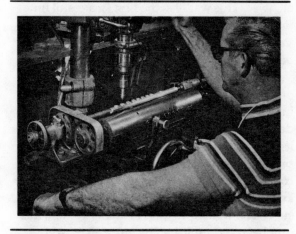

Figure 17

Keys were formerly pounded out by hand (sometimes, as in France, their manufacture was a cottage industry) but now are drop-forged by machine with a pressure of about 100 tons. These keys are then soldered to the hinge tubing. If the flute is to be plated, the tubes and keys are immersed in a chemical bath. The flute is then assembled with completed key mechanism, springs, and pads.

Wooden Boehm flutes are still found in England, Germany and the adjacent Low Countries, and Eastern Europe. (In these areas, cheaper flutes are also sometimes made of ebonite, a hard-rubber compound resembling ebony.) While the processes by which metal flute bodies are made have become increasingly mechanized, wooden flutemakers use nearly

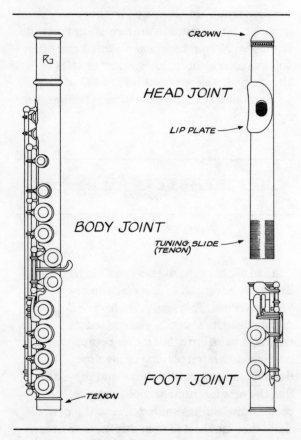

Figure 16

the same techniques as their predecessors two hundred years ago.

The seasoned wood—usually African blackwood (grenadilla)—is first cleaved or sawed into approximately shaped pieces. The pieces are turned on a lathe roughly to shape, given a preliminary bore, and set aside for more seasoning—often using steam and dry heat to speed the process.

The piece is then returned to the lathe, where the outside is turned to final shape and the bore is carefully developed with various bits and reamers. Afterward, it receives another long seasoning in an oil bath. Finally, the holes are drilled and counterbored, the pillars are screwed in, and the flute is assembled.

Flute-making centers of the world include the United States—with a concentration in Elkhart, Indiana—England, France, and Germany. More recently, Japan and other Far Eastern countries have also begun manufacturing flutes, largely for export to Western nations.

Looking Ahead

It is interesting to note that the Boehm flute—which we think of as *the* flute—is only a century and a quarter old, not as old yet as the Baroque flute was when supplanted by the Boehm instrument. Despite the brilliance of its design and its total ascendancy in our culture, there is no guarantee that it will be the final form of the flute in the West. In fact, we can be almost positive that it won't. Instruments change according to the requirements of the music that is played on them, and that music is in continual evolution. Someday—who knows how soon?—a new form of flute will have to be designed to meet the demands of a new music. But for now . . .

Part II

 Selection and Care

3

Finding Your Flute

The more you know about flutes, and the more sensitive you are to them, the more likely you are to wind up with the right one for you. There are a number of ways of finding a flute to start playing. One of the most common, of course, is to buy one from a music store. One advantage of this is that you can compare and choose from a variety of flutes. Many music stores also sell reconditioned flutes or demonstrator models, which can be good bargains.

It is best to buy from a music store that has its own repair facilities and one that will guarantee the flute for a period of time. Most new flutes come with a guarantee from the maker, but this can mean you have to send the instrument back to the factory for a three-minute adjustment!

Many music stores have band instrument rental programs. Renting a flute at first can give you a chance to try out flute playing, and the particular flute, without making a heavy financial commitment. Most stores will apply at least part of the rental to an eventual purchase, usually at secondhand prices.

Used flutes can be found through newspaper ads, music school bulletin boards, pawn shops, flea markets, etc. Some incredible bargains can be discovered this way. When you inspect the flute, however, it is important to know exactly what you're doing or to bring along someone who does.

Or you may have a friend who owns a flute that's not being used and who is willing to loan it to you. There's no more economical way to start on the flute!

Buying Name Brands

With flutes, buying by name is generally a good practice, since the reputations of the better-known companies have been built by the quality of their products. Though there may be little difference between these flutes and the lesser-known brands in terms of sound and acoustic design, over a long period you will

CROWN

HEAD JOINT

LIP PLATE

BODY JOINT

TUNING SLIDE (TENON)

FOOT JOINT

TENON

Figure 18

often find a difference in the durability of the instrument. (This general rule is no longer fully reliable, due to the growing takeover of manufacturers by large corporations, but it should remain true for most of the best-known companies.) Among North American companies, the reputable companies include Armstrong, Artley, and Gemeinhardt; in the handmade flute category, Haynes and Powell are well-known names. In Europe the list includes Couesnon, Hammig, Marigaux, Monnig, Selmer, U.S.A., and Rudall, Carte. In Japan, Yamaha and Muramatsu are considered good.*

Metal Flutes— the Flute Hierarchy

There is a definite hierarchy of metal flute models, based mainly on the materials used and the care with which the flutes are made. As you go up the scale of metals, the quality of construction increases, and so does the price.

The least expensive flute, called a *student model*, is made from nickel-silver (also called *German silver*). Nickel-silver actually has no silver in it at all—it is an alloy of copper, zinc, and nickel. If well made and properly cared for, a flute of this type can last a very long time.

Student flutes are covered, or *plated*, with a layer of either nickel or silver, to help resist corrosion. Silver plating lasts longer, gives a smoother, less metallic tone, is less slippery to hold, and can be reapplied when the original plating wears through. The only advantage to nickel plating is that it stays shiny with very little maintenance. Since the extra cost of silver plating is very small, it is preferable to the nickel.

Moving up the hierarchy of models, silver— with its slightly deeper, richer tone and slightly better "response"—replaces the other metals for more and more parts of the flute. The next step above a student flute is one in which the

head joint is made of silver. Since the influence of the material on the flute occurs mainly at the head joint, this gives the flute basically the characteristics of a silver flute. The next level up is an all-silver body, and the one above that has a silver key mechanism as well.

Many times someone selling a flute secondhand assumes it is silver but actually has no idea what it is made of. Usually a flute says right on it if any portion of it is silver. Other ways to tell are: ask the original price; check the tenons, to see if silver plating has worn through; see whether it is nickel-plated—if the flute is nickel-plated, there is no silver in it.

Above the all-silver flutes in the hierarchy there is still one more large step—the handmade flutes. Most of these are made in silver, but gold and platinum are also available. Gold gives a "warmer," "richer" sound than silver, with somewhat less carrying power. Platinum, first used because it would theoretically make the best flute material, has a tone generally considered "cold."

Wooden Flutes

Modern flutes made from wood are still common in some parts of Europe (Britain, Germany and the Low Countries, and Eastern Europe).* African blackwood (grenadilla) is the most common wood used; formerly, cocuswood was predominant, but it is no longer available in the finer grades. Pieces for the less expensive flutes are sawed from the log, while for the most expensive models they are cleaved. Cleaving exposes defects in the wood that can be rejected at this early stage, partially safeguarding against cracking in the finished flute. Cleaving also guarantees that the grain will run end-to-end in the flute, which is preferable acoustically. Student models are sometimes made from ebonite, a hard-rubber compound resembling ebony, which is moisture-proof, but not heat-proof.

Because of the greater "resistance" of the wooden flute body, a wooden flute requires a

---

*This list should not be regarded as definitive, especially for areas outside of North America. It is meant merely as an aid to those who have no other way of acquiring reliable advice concerning flute manufacturers.

---

*In the United States, modern wooden flutes are being crafted by Brannen Brothers Flutemakers, Littleton Road, Harvard, Massachusetts 01451.

tighter, more "muscular" blowing style. This generally produces a tone that is more rich, solid, and powerful than that normally produced on the metal flute. Disadvantages are that this type of blowing makes subtlety in playing more difficult to achieve and tires out the lips more quickly.

Various "compromises" between the wooden and the metal flute are available. Wooden flutes are made with thinned bodies and/or head joints to provide some of the tonal properties of wood with less resistance. Both wooden and metal flutes can be fitted with head joints of the other material.* (As stated before, the material's influence on the flute's characteristics occurs mainly at the head joint.)

Flute Quality—General

Though quality of construction is generally related to brand name and to position in the flute "hierarchy," the sound and playing properties of a flute don't necessarily follow the hierarchical pattern. These properties are determined mainly at the mouth hole, and the dimensions of this part of the flute are so critical that no two flutes ever sound or play exactly alike. So, while it's a good idea to buy according to name and hierarchy, you should also choose on the basis of the individual flute.

I should state here that a beginner does not need a top-quality flute. The respect due to a superior instrument demands that it be reserved for someone with a developed skill and a deep commitment. Generally, you are ready for a finer flute when you find it makes a difference in your playing.

Plateau Model, French Model

Two models of the modern flute are manufactured today: the *plateau model* and the *French model*. (In Germany, Italy, and Eastern Europe, the French model is not generally

available; in France, it is practically the only one used.) The main difference between the two is that the French, or *open-hole,* model has holes in the centers of five of the keys (see figure 19).

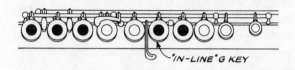

Figure 19

There are several advantages to this: the holes are said to give a very slightly clearer, louder sound, because the air vibrations are less muffled; some of the third octave notes have slightly better tuning; and on some notes, extra effects can be achieved by half-holing—covering only half the hole of a depressed key, in order to bend the note sharp. These effects are especially useful in some styles of jazz or in imitating various kinds of foreign music.

On the open-hole flute, when you press down one of the open keys, you must also close off the center hole with your finger so that no air can escape. This requires more strictness in the holding position, which you might consider either an advantage or a disadvantage.

Another difference between the two models is that the French model usually has a G key in line with the rest of the keys, while the G key on the plateau model is "offset" slightly (compare figures 18 and 19). Though the in-line G has the advantage of "forcing" the left hand into a proper, vertical position, it is actually a somewhat clumsy arrangement; the offset G fits the hand much better.

The French model flute is slightly more expensive, both in initial purchase price and in maintenance costs.

Other Options and Variations

B foot joint. This style, available in most countries, has an extra key on the foot joint, enabling the flutist to play one note lower in the first octave (see figure 20).

---

*In the United States, custom-fitted wooden head joints can now be obtained from the following: Alexander Eppler (recommended), 1921 5th Avenue, Seattle, Washington 98101; and Diamond Cutler Fluteworks, 891 12th Street, Boulder, Colorado 80302.

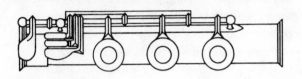

Figure 20

Thin-wall construction (metal flute). The thinner walls give a higher, thinner sound that is more responsive but somewhat harder to control.

Open G-sharp key. This key arrangement is commonly found in Eastern Europe. The lever played by the left little finger closes its hole when pressed, rather than opening the hole, as on most current-day flutes. This is the form of the mechanism that originally appeared on the modern flute, and a good case can be made for its superiority.

Features to Look For

There are several features you should look for on a flute, especially if you are buying a new instrument.

Curved lip plate (metal flute). This makes for easier blowing. (See figure 21.)

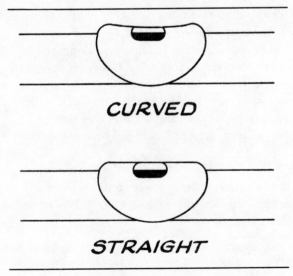

CURVED

STRAIGHT

Figure 21

Mouth hole—average size. The two basic shapes used for the mouth hole are the oval and the rounded rectangle; either one is acceptable. The size of the mouth hole, however, should not vary too much from the average. A large mouth hole will favor the low notes at the expense of the high, while a small mouth hole will favor the high notes at the expense of the low.

Integral, rolled tone holes (metal flute). The walls of the holes should be raised directly from the body of the flute, instead of being soldered on, to reduce the chance of having air leaks. An exception is made in the case of some handmade flutes. These are normally fashioned with thinner metal tubing, so most makers do not raise the hole walls from the tube itself.

The tops of the holes should be curled, or "rolled," so that no sharp edge is presented to the pad (see figure 22)—this increases pad life. (Some flutes have tone holes that are integral but not rolled.)

"OLD-STYLE"

INTEGRAL ROLLED TONE HOLE

Figure 22

Rib-and-post construction (metal flute). In this style of construction, the posts that hold the key mechanism are not soldered directly to the body but instead to strips of metal (ribs) that are then soldered to the body (see figure 23). This greatly increases the reliability of the key mechanism.

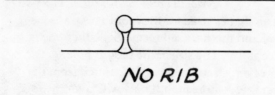

NO RIB

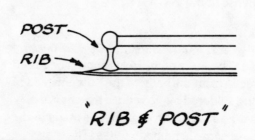

POST

RIB

"RIB & POST"

Figure 23

Regulating screws. These are shown in figure 24. They allow the flutist to make basic adjustments to the flute mechanism (see chapter 4), decreasing the need for professional attention. The flute should have four or five regulating screws; flutes with more than five screws have a tendency to go out of adjustment too easily. Handmade flutes do not normally have regulating screws.

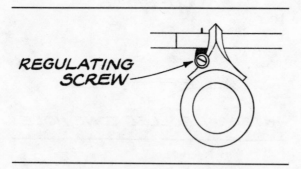

REGULATING SCREW

Figure 24

Pitch standard. A series of conferences in the first half of this century raised the international standard pitch from A = 435 vibrations per second, to A = 440. This was accomplished in the United States and England in 1920 and in continental Europe in 1939—with the exception of France, which still retains the previous standard. This means that flutes made in those areas before the dates given will be tuned slightly below today's standard pitch and are therefore not useful in group playing (unless modified by a competent repair shop). The same applies to French flutes played outside of France.

Revised scale. The completely new acoustic proportions that the flute requires because of the pitch change discussed above are only now being introduced into flute manufacture. (Flutes made during this transition period have been more-or-less jury-rigged affairs.) The difference will show up in improved internal tuning, evenness of tone, and better responsiveness when playing at concert pitch. It will probably take some time, though, before all flute manufacturers convert to the new dimensions.*

Checking Out a Used Flute

If you are buying a secondhand flute, the list below will help you to determine its condition. Unless you are familiar with flutes, however, I strongly recommend that you bring along someone who is, to help you evaluate it. Or you could bring the instrument to a repair shop for a professional judgment.

Keep in mind that, although some flutes are truly beyond repair, most faulty conditions can be and are corrected during a standard overhaul in any repair shop. (More on overhauls in chapter 4.) In fact, the best bargains can often be found among flutes that "don't work"—they sometimes require only a simple regulating adjustment, accomplished in a few moments.

Pads. These are the soft inserts in the keys that actually make contact with the holes. They should not be torn or yellowed and dried out.

---

* At this writing, the only companies known to me to be manufacturing revised scale flutes are Yamaha and Armstrong. Some handmade flutes are made to the revised scale.

Springs. These should be strong enough so that the keys return to resting position with a firm motion.

Action. The action should have a solid feeling. There should be free movement of all keys. No key "clicks" should be heard. Try wiggling the keys sideways—there should be very little movement.

Tenons. The joints should fit together snugly, but not tightly. There should be no side play when the instrument is assembled.

Head joint cork. Try pulling straight out on the crown (the piece at the very top). If it moves, the cork inside is too loose.

Mouth hole. This should have *no* nicks or scratches, especially on the edge you blow toward. This repair is *expensive.*

Dents (metal flute). Small dents on the body will have almost no effect, but dents on the head joint can cause tuning problems.

Finish (metal flute). The condition of the finish has no effect on the playing of the flute.

Cracked body (wood flute). This can be repaired.

Warped body (wood, ebonite). This can be repaired on an ebonite flute, not on a

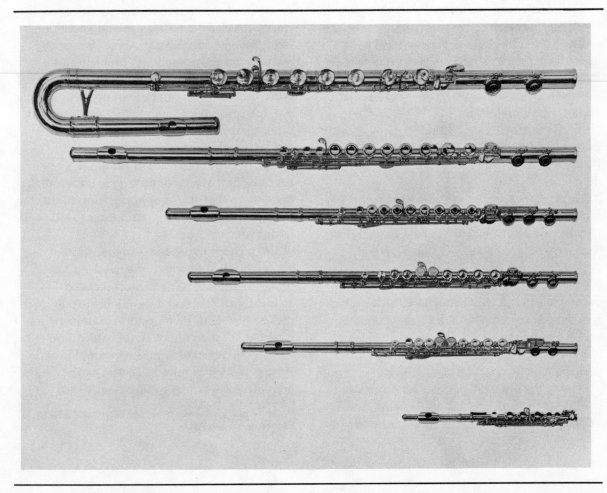

Figure 25
From bottom to top: piccolo; E-flat flute; soprano flute; soprano flute, B foot joint; alto flute; and bass flute

wooden one. A slight curving is to be expected on all older wooden flutes.

Other Sizes of Flutes

Modern flutes are actually made in several different sizes. The one with which we are most familiar—the *soprano* or *concert* flute—is considered musically the most versatile and satisfactory, and it is therefore by far the most commonly used. Other sizes, however, are useful for special purposes.

The alto flute is wider and longer than the soprano and starts a half octave below it, on G. Its tone is very rich and mellow. Because of the larger volume of air, it requires more breath and is slower to respond. (This size of flute was previously referred to as *bass,* and in Europe it is still sometimes mistakenly called by this name.)

The bass flute starts one more half octave below the alto, on C. It is so long that the head joint has to be curved a full 180 degrees to allow the flutist to reach the mouth hole. Its tone is extremely deep, and even more breath is required than on the alto.

The E-flat flute is a slightly smaller version of the soprano. Its main use is for children whose hands are not yet large enough for a standard flute.

The piccolo is a small flute with a high, shrill tone. Most piccolos are made in the key of C, playing one octave higher than the concert flute; another type, the D-flat piccolo—formerly popular but now becoming obsolete—plays one note higher. There are two major models of the piccolo: the metal cylindrical-bore model, which is easier to blow and has more stable intonation; and the wooden, conical-bore model, which is less shrill. Various combinations are also available.

Playing the piccolo requires a very tight holding of the lips, and a careful attention to intonation; you will find it difficult to switch between piccolo and flute unless you regularly devote time to each. When buying a student model, make sure it has been designed so that you can close all keys without hitting others.

The fingerings for all these flutes are basically the same as on the concert flute, but transposition is necessary when reading music. (See chapter 15 on reading music.)

Electronic Amplification

Flutes can be amplified by microphone or by pickup. There are advantages to each method. A microphone gives you a certain degree of flexibility by allowing you to move closer and farther away. You can go all the way from a low, breathy tone played close to the mike to shrieking high notes played from a distance, all without touching a control.

Pickups also have strong advantages. You don't have to worry about where you are in relation to a mike. Feedback problems are reduced or eliminated. Often the pickup is used with a preamp that can be kept near you, giving you full control over your own volume output. The pickup can be easily hooked through various electronic special effect devices. Probably most important of all, the reproduction quality of pickups is substantially better than that of microphones. In fact, this can even be a disadvantage—it's harder to hide your faults from a pickup.

The pickups in use today are electronic assemblies that fit within the head joint itself, replacing the cork. The various pickups available are based on differing principles, each pickup having its own peculiar characteristics. If possible, try out various types before buying.*

For good reproduction, a *voice* amplification system or PA is required. Electric guitar amplifiers will not reproduce clearly.

---

*Current manufacturers in the United States are FRAP, Barcus-Berry, and ATD.

4
Caring for Your Flute

The flute is a very delicate instrument and cannot play well if it is not properly cared for. Even a slight deterioration can create conditions that will hinder the flow of your music through the instrument. It is very important, then, to keep your flute in good condition. Even before you begin playing, you should learn how to assemble and disassemble your flute properly.

Assembly, Playing, Disassembly

The best way to grip the joints for assembly is to hold them without touching the key mechanism at all. If you can't manage that, at least put as little pressure on the mechanism as possible. It is fairly easy to push the key mechanism out of adjustment, which can make playing difficult or impossible.

Assemble the joints with a twisting motion, as shown in figure 26. Do not jockey the joints from side to side, as this may bend the connecting (metal) tenons. The tenons should fit into their sockets just snugly; they should not be so tight that the joints have to be forced into position. On the other hand, a tenon that is too loose will leak air, making playing more difficult. (Treatments for tight and loose tenons are discussed later in this chapter.)

Always hold the flute with the keys pointing upward, to prevent the moisture of your playing from running over the pads. During a playing session, avoid eating or drinking, especially anything sweet, and also avoid smoking—any of these will create a buildup on the pads that will cause sticking. (The acid from cigarette smoke will also eat into the blowing edge of the mouth hole.)

Follow the same rules for taking apart your flute that you used for assembling it. Then wipe the moisture out of the flute. The main purpose of this is to prevent the pads from becoming damp, either from moisture running over them directly, or from too much humidity in the case. Dampness causes the pads to expand and go out of adjustment to their holes. On a wooden flute, wiping also distributes the moisture more evenly, to prevent cracking and warping.

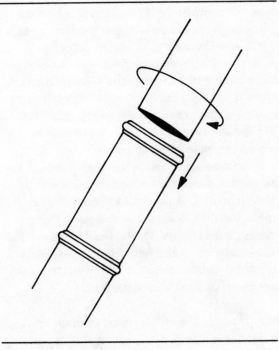

Figure 26

To wipe out the flute, use a soft cloth hooked through the cleaning rod found in your case. (If you don't have a cleaning rod, you can buy one separately or make one from a slotted wooden dowel.) It is not necessary to dry out the inside completely; it can remain slightly damp. The cloth should not be left inside the case, as this defeats much of the purpose of the wiping.

Some flutes come with protective caps to place over the tenons. The original purpose of these was to protect *the case* from the lubrication of the tenons. Since metal tenons should receive no lubrication (see the next section below), these caps are better left unused.

When the flute is in its case, the cover should be kept closed to keep dust out of the key mechanism; it should also be latched, so that the flute won't tumble out if anyone picks up the case. When you are in a public place, you should not leave your flute unattended, as flute theft is very common.

Minor Maintenance

Cleaning. Tarnishing is caused by pollution in the air and by the perspiration of the flutist. It does no real harm and is impossible to stop in any case, so you may ignore it completely. If you wish to retard the process, the best way is to give the flute a quick rubdown with a soft cloth after each playing.

To give the flute a more thorough cleaning, use a cloth soaked with warm water or alcohol. *Never use polish*—this can easily work into the key mechanism and wear it down. Any dust around the keys can be removed with a small watercolor paintbrush.

A cloth soaked in water or alcohol should also be used occasionally to clean the inside of the mouth hole. (Q-tips should not be used on metal mouth holes, as they will leave slight dents on the surface.) Metal head joints can be washed in water and mild soap, if the cork is removed. (Instructions for taking out the cork are given later in this chapter.)

Tenons. The most common cause of a tight assembly is dirty tenons. It is important, then, on both metal and wooden flutes, to keep the tenons and their sockets wiped clean. This will keep them working freely and prevent a buildup of dirt from acting as an abrasive. (A Q-tip can be used to clean the sockets.) Wooden tenons should occasionally be lubricated with a light coating of lapping grease (cork grease). *No oil or grease should be applied to metal tenons*—this attracts dust, which then acts as an abrasive. (Further treatment for tight and loose tenons is described in the section on repairs below.)

Oiling. The key mechanism should be oiled once or twice a year—more often, if you live in a humid or salty climate. Use a light lubricating oil, such as woodwind key oil or sewing machine oil. Apply the oil at every break in the hinge tubing, on the regulating screws, and on the springs (to resist corrosion). Apply as little oil as possible, using the end of a needle or pointed toothpick—it is very easy to overdo it. Be sure to keep the oil off the pads. As you oil each spot, move the keys up and down so the oil will work in. Blot off all excess with newsprint, cigarette paper, or blotting paper.

Head Joint Cork

Placement. The head joint cork is placed in a certain position to bring the notes of the flute into tune *with each other;* any shifting of this cork will throw off the internal tuning of the instrument. *Do not move the cork to tune to other instruments.* (Tuning to other instruments is covered in chapter 10.)

To check whether your cork is placed properly, insert the notched end of your cleaning rod all the way into the head joint. If the cork is in the correct position, the notch will appear in the exact center of the mouth hole (as shown in figure 27).* If you don't have a cleaning rod, you can make a gauge from a dowel or rod. The measurement from the notch to the end of the rod that touches the cork is 17 millimeters or about 11/16 inch. (If you have a cleaning rod, you might check it against this

---

* Actually, unless your flute is built on a revised scale (see chapter 3), you may be able to improve its internal tuning at concert pitch by moving the cork just slightly farther from the mouth hole. Experiment and see how this works for you.

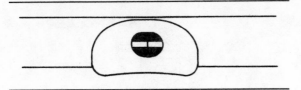

Figure 27

measurement, as these rods are not always accurately marked.)

To pull the cork farther away from the mouth hole, simply screw in the crown, turning it clockwise as you look on it from the top (see figure 28). To move the cork in toward the mouth hole, unscrew the crown a little (turn it counterclockwise), and shove it in with the ball of your hand. (You can see how the cork mechanism works if you unscrew the crown completely and look inside.) After adjustment, the crown should be left screwed securely against the head joint.

If the cork hasn't been moved in a long time it may be "frozen" in place. In this case, you may have to break it loose by shoving it inward before you can draw it farther toward the top. (See below for further steps in this procedure.)

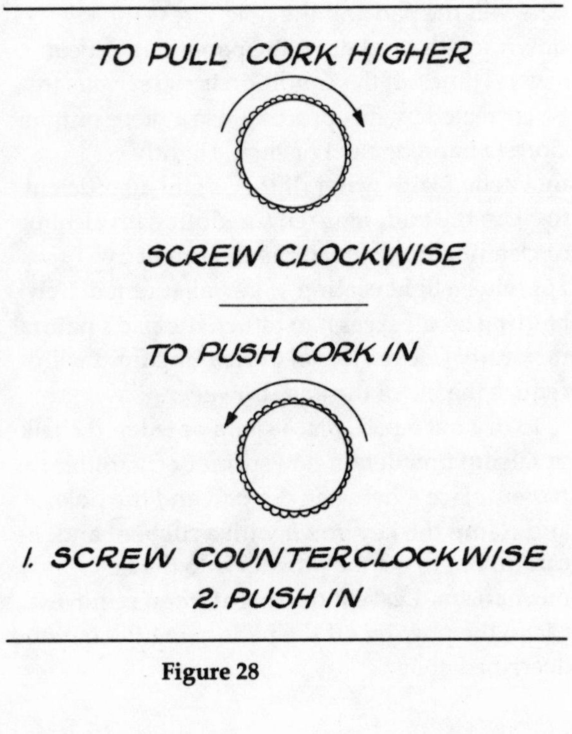

Removal. The head joint cork may have to be removed for work on the cork itself or to clean the head joint. First move the cork closer to the mouth hole, as instructed above, then unscrew the crown completely, and use your cleaning rod to push the cork out through the tuning slide (head joint tenon), as noted in figure 29. The cork *must* leave and enter by this end, because the head joint is tapered narrower at the top.

Loose and tight corks. For the flute to play properly, the cork must absolutely be airtight, when it is in place in the head joint. Test this by pulling straight up on the crown: if the cork moves, it is too loose. Sometimes the cork can be expanded by screwing the top metal plate tighter onto the cork. (See figure 30.) Another way is to apply a *light* coating of cork grease (lapping grease) or tallow to the cork. If neither method does the trick, the cork should probably be replaced. (Passing the cork over a flame—the method used by some repair shops—is not a permanent solution.)

If you are trying to adjust the cork placement and the cork won't move, *do not try to force it higher up the flute.* You can actually stretch a metal head joint or crack a wooden one this way. Remove the crown, and place a hollow rod over the screw rod (you can use a dowel with a hole drilled in it, the tube of a ballpoint pen, or a

TO PULL CORK HIGHER

SCREW CLOCKWISE

TO PUSH CORK IN

I. SCREW COUNTERCLOCKWISE
2. PUSH IN

Figure 28

CORK MUST LEAVE BY THIS END ⟶

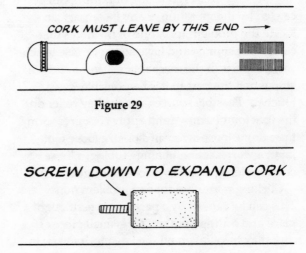

Figure 29

SCREW DOWN TO EXPAND CORK

Figure 30

similar implement). Use this to drive the cork out through the tuning slide.

You can then "loosen" the cork with a *light* application of cork grease. (Cork grease corrects both tight and loose corks, because it both seals and lubricates.) If this is insufficient, you can try sanding it down a little, but make sure the sanding is done *evenly*.

Repairs

Of the various problems that can occur on the flute, some can be corrected by the player, and others are best left to a repair shop. Both kinds are discussed here. In general, the average player is not advised to attempt any repairs that require taking apart the key mechanism. (For those wishing to pursue flute repair further, sources are given in the reading list at the end of this book.)

Tight and loose tenons. If tenons become tight, all that may be required is cleaning and/or lubrication, as described earlier in this chapter. If metal tenons require more than this to correct tightness or looseness they must be dealt with by a repair shop.

A loose wooden tenon can be tightened by winding a few turns of lapping thread (hemp) around it. Loosening can be done by light, *even* sanding, followed by a reapplication of lapping grease.

Noises. Buzzing or rattling can be caused by the vibration of any loose part. To locate the problem, play one of the notes that causes the sound, and have someone else touch various parts of the mechanism. The sound will stop when the part that is responsible is touched. Possible sources are: the key roller on the foot joint (remove and apply cork grease on the axle); a loose screw in a post; a loose foot joint; a worn section of hinge tubing; a loose screw holding a pad in place. (See figure 31.)

Clicking is another type of problem noise. This can be caused by a part that is bent out of place and hitting another. Or a small piece of cork may have fallen off the key mechanism; in this case, you will usually see one or two keys

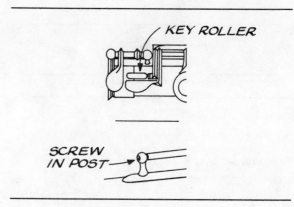

Figure 31

resting much higher off their holes than the others are.

Most of the conditions causing noises are best left to a repair shop.

Sticking keys. If a key is slow to come up (return to resting position), this could have several causes. The key mechanism may need oiling. The key's axle may have become bent. If the key remains down for a split second, then pops up with a smacking sound, the pad is sticking on the rim of the note hole. This can be caused by humidity or by grime on the pads.

To clean a pad, place a blank piece of newspaper, a cigarette paper, or some thin cloth between the pad and the hole. Press the key down solidly, and draw the paper out; repeat several times. If the condition is too serious to be corrected by this process, use a piece of thin cloth (a handkerchief or such) slightly moistened with water. If this is still insufficient to clean the pad, moisten the cloth with alcohol or cleaning fluid; finish the treatment by applying a light coating of key oil (immediately blotting off all excess) to return the pad's natural moisture. Use of alcohol or cleaning fluid will reduce the life of the pad, however.

To dry out a pad, place some powdered chalk or talcum powder on newsprint or cigarette paper, place it between the pad and the hole, and clamp the key down with a rubber band. Be careful not to get the powder into the key mechanism. Leave it overnight, then remove it. Clean the powder off the pads using the method described above.

Springs. A key hanging loose indicates trouble with a spring. Figure 32 shows a typical spring mechanism. The spring itself is made from wire of nickel-silver, gold, or stainless steel, or from blued-steel needles. (Steel needles are no longer used on American flutes.)

If one of your keys goes out of commission, look for the spring that works on it. If the spring is broken, or bent sharply, it will have to be replaced by a repair shop. (Steel springs are especially prone to breaking, due to rust.) It may, however, simply be off its hook, in which case you can push it back into place. The best tool to use for this is a small crocheting hook; you can make the hook even handier by filing a V-shaped notch in the top (see figure 33).

If the spring has worked loose from its post, you may be able to simply push it back in, at least as a temporary remedy. If your springs are made of one of the soft wires, flatten the post end by squeezing it with a pair of pliers (see figure 34); this will make it wedge more tightly into the post. Make sure when you push the

spring back in that you get the curve in a plane parallel to the flute.

If a spring is too weak (as it may well be when you reattach it), unhook it and give it a curving bend, in the same direction as it presses against its spring hook. Be careful not to get a sharp bend in it.

If a spring breaks at a critical time, you may be able to hook up a small rubber band as a temporary substitute. Some performers carry several in their cases for just this purpose. (Remove the bands as soon as possible, however, since the sulphur in the rubber corrodes metal.)

Regulation and "leaky" pads. When a note doesn't play properly, or when you have to press a key down hard to get the sound, it means that one or more keys aren't sealing off their holes properly. This usually affects not only the individual note, but also every other note below it on the flute. If you have a whole series of bad notes, then, you can often locate the one leaking key that is responsible by seeing where the notes start "going off."

Improper seals can be caused by individual pads leaking at some point along their rims or more often by defects in the regulation—the adjustments between keys that work together. Most flutes have regulating screws, in order to allow these adjustments to be made easily. (If your flute doesn't have them, you will not be able to regulate the flute yourself.) To do the regulation, you need a jeweler's screwdriver and a "feeler gauge" made from a narrow strip of newsprint or cigarette paper.

One area on the flute commonly requiring regulation is the four keys at the bottom of the body joint (see figure 35). To regulate them, press down the key nearest to the foot joint. Adjust the regulating screw on that key until it looks as if the two keys that go down are hitting the rims of their note holes at the same time. Take your feeler gauge and slip an end of it under the first key, close the key with a moderate pressure, and pull out the gauge, feeling how much pull you need to get it out. Now slip it under the other key and press down again on the *first key*—the same key as before—

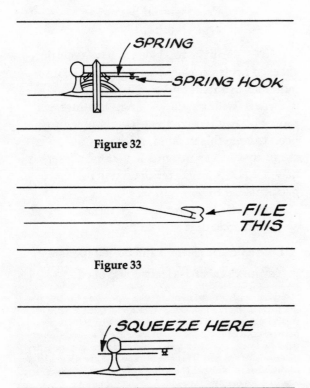

Figure 32

Figure 33

Figure 34

with the same amount of pressure (see figure 36); pull the feeler out again. If it took more or less pull to get out than under the first key, adjust the regulating screw until both keys have about the same amount of "drag."

Do the same for the next two keys. The notes that can be played to test these regulations are F-sharp, alternate F-sharp (see chapter 11), and F, respectively. The third key will also move an extra key, closer to the top of the flute. There may or may not be a regulating screw for this adjustment; if so, it will be found on the back of the flute. The test note for this combination is B-flat.

Another combination with a regulating screw is found closer to the top of the flute. This is adjusted in the same way, and is checked using the note A (see figure 37). Additional regulating screws are found on some flutes.

If regulation keeps going out of adjustment because of loose regulating screws, put nail polish on the screws to hold them in place. (It

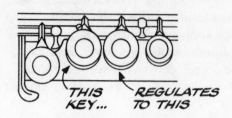

Figure 37

can easily be removed later with nail polish remover.) Some key combinations are regulated by cork; in these cases, it is sometimes possible to regulate by adding a piece of tape to the cork. The keys on the foot joint often go out of adjustment, but there is no simple way for the flutist to adjust them.

If regulation doesn't seem to correct the problem, some individual pads are probably leaking. You can test this by using your feeler gauge at various points around the rim of the pad; if there is little or no drag at some spots, the pad is leaking at those points. This problem should be corrected by a repair shop.

Professional Servicing and Overhaul

It is a good idea to have your flute checked professionally once or twice a year for minor adjustments and an oiling. Every one to five years (with regular playing), the flute will probably require a complete overhaul. Flutists need to keep this in mind, since the flute goes out of condition so gradually that the player may not notice any deterioration in its performance.*

A complete flute overhaul, or reconditioning, should include the following:

1. Entire flute is cleaned and buffed (polished).

2. Key mechanism is cleaned and oiled.

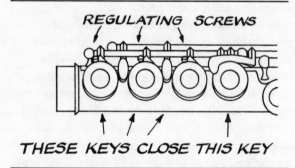

Figure 35

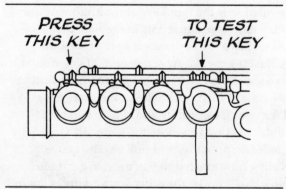

Figure 36

---

*I am currently experimenting with extending the life of my pads using the following method: Moisten a piece of cigarette paper with woodwind key oil. Place the paper between the pad and the rim of the note hole, and press the key down. *Immediately* remove the paper and use a dry piece to blot the pad. This can be repeated approximately once a year. It replaces the natural oiliness of the pads, and loss of oil is the main cause of pad deterioration.

How is it working for me? So far so good. But it's strictly an experiment—proceed at your own risk!

3. Springs are strengthened or replaced, as necessary.

4. Excessive sideways motion is taken out of keys.

5. New corks are placed on the keys.

6. New pads are installed.

7. Thorough regulation of keys is made.

8. The head joint cork is adjusted or replaced, as necessary.

No reconditioning job is acceptable unless all notes play with only light *pressure on the keys.* A student flute is not likely to receive as careful attention as a finer instrument would, but the condition stated above is an absolute minimum expectation. If you play a high-quality flute, you should probably request that the mouth hole not be buffed, as this eventually wears down the blowing edge.

Servicing a flute is a very sensitive job, and not all repair shops are equally competent or concerned about it. To locate a good repair shop, ask woodwind musicians, especially performers and teachers, if possible. You should have no trouble getting reliable guidance in this way, as shops usually develop strong reputations. The average player, however, has no need of flute specialists who charge above-standard rates.*

---

*In the United States, if you cannot find a suitable repair shop near you, you may want to use Armstrong's mail order repair service. For details, write W. T. Armstrong Company, P.O. Box 963, Elkhart, Indiana 46514.

Part III

Flute Technique

5

Embouchure and Breath

Getting a Sound—Basic Embouchure

Getting a sound on the flute is easy! Take just the head joint, lay your lower lip over the edge of the mouth hole, and blow it like a pop bottle.

Did you get it? What's that you say? You've never blown on a pop bottle? All right then, let's go at it another way. The following is a description of the basic flute *embouchure*—the way you hold your lips and mouth while playing.* Looking in a mirror will be helpful.

The mouth hole of the flute should be pointed directly upward, and your head should be held straight up. Lay your bottom lip *loosely* over the edge of the mouth hole—not pulled up, or curled under itself, or pressed down hard against the flute. It should cover about a quarter of the mouth hole.

Now, press your lips together at the corners and sides, leaving a roughly oval opening at the front of your mouth. Center this opening above the mouth hole (even if the opening isn't in the exact center of your mouth). Point your lips diagonally downward, and blow a solid stream of air directly at the opposite edge of the mouth hole. Don't lift up your bottom lip as you blow!

The instructions for a wooden flute embouchure are slightly different from those given above. The wooden flute requires a more "muscular" embouchure in order to bring out its rich and powerful tone. The bottom lip is pressed hard against the head joint (instead of being relaxed), and the corners of the lips are drawn back more tightly.

If your blowing produces no sound, check your bottom lip to make sure you're not unconsciously pulling it up. Rotate the flute to

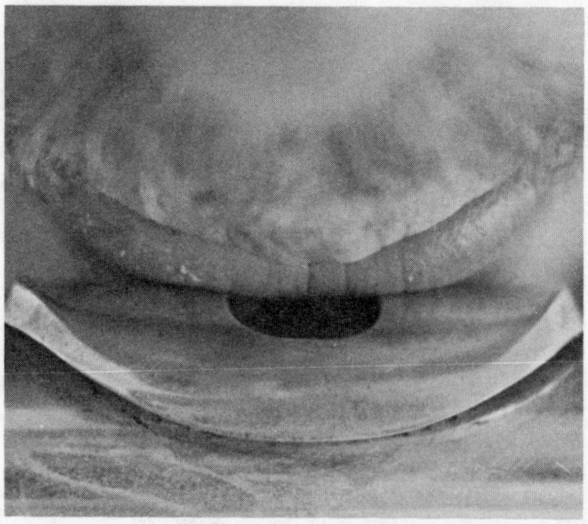

Figure 38

Embouchure can also be used to refer to the mouth hole of the flute or to the physiological structure of the individual player's mouth. This book mostly avoids those uses, to eliminate confusion.

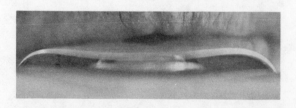

Figure 39

change the angle at which your breath hits the blowing edge. Also, try varying the shape and pressure of your blowing, and how far your bottom lip extends over the hole. On the metal flute, *make sure your bottom lip is relaxed*— pressing it down will tire your lips very quickly. It's best to try for only brief periods and come back to it frequently. Dizziness and tingling feelings in your limbs are normal at this stage; use them as a signal to rest.

After you get the initial sound, keep the head joint handy and blow it at odd moments to help you gain consistency.

Basic Breathing

A major part of flute playing is learning to manage the flow of breath from your body into the body of the flute. Much of the expressiveness of your music will come from the degree of control and flexibility you have in your breathing.

In flute playing, breathing is done mainly from the diaphragm, a muscle that extends horizontally across the bottom of the chest and presses against the bottom of the lungs. To find your diaphragm, push your stomach way out as you breathe in; then pull it way in as you breathe out. (Make sure you're not getting the directions backward!) The muscle that does that is the diaphragm, as it moves down to allow the lungs to fill (stomach out), then up to squeeze air out of them (stomach in).

Here is an exercise to give you the feel for proper breathing: Stand erect, holding your elbows away from your body. Now push your diaphragm straight down, and your chest muscles slightly outward. The sensation should be that your entire upper body is a bellows that's filling up, evenly and all at once. Your stomach should *not* protrude very far forward, as it did in

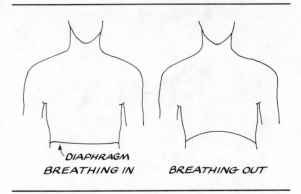

DIAPHRAGM
BREATHING IN   BREATHING OUT

Figure 40

the initial exercise given above. Instead, there should be a slight expansion in the stomach, and a similar expansion in the small of the back, directly behind it. An even smaller expansion should be felt around the chest, in the front and back. There will be a *very* slight raising of the shoulders, but this should come only as a result of the chest expansion, without any movement of the shoulder muscles themselves.

Fill your lungs only as much as is comfortable, then exhale by reversing the above instructions. When you have the feel of the breathing, use it while blowing a note on your head joint.

Though this is actually a very natural way of breathing, many people do not normally breathe fully, and they may have trouble with it at first. You may have to build up the strength of your diaphragm slowly over a period of time. The extra oxygen in your system may cause dizziness and tingling feelings in your limbs, especially the hands. This is called *hyperventilation*. Beginning players usually aggravate the condition by using much more air than is necessary to produce the sound. Hyperventilation will stop bothering you as you get used to the extra air in your lungs and learn to blow more efficiently.

6
Posture

In flute playing, posture is the efficient use of the body. Its one purpose is to make the production of music as effortless as possible, in order to allow full play to your creativity. Posture includes every element of how you hold yourself and how you hold your flute. It must constitute a unit, each part contributing to the whole. Correct posture is an outgrowth of a deep sympathy for the instrument and its requirements, as well as the requirements of your own body.

A flutist's posture is built on three major principles:

1. Minimum restriction of breathing,
2. Maximum facility of finger movement, and
3. Minimum muscular effort.

Keep these principles in mind, and use them as criteria for judging any point of posture about which you have a question.

Flute Assembly and Hand Position

Begin this consideration of posture by assembling your flute. Read carefully the instructions for assembly in chapter 4; then put your flute together using the alignment shown in figure 41. (You may be adjusting that alignment later.) Push the head joint all the way in, then pull it out again about ⅛ inch (3 millimeters).

Hold the flute pointing to the right, with your hands in the position shown in figure 42, and place your fingers on the keys as shown on

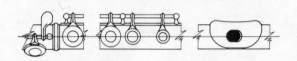

Figure 41

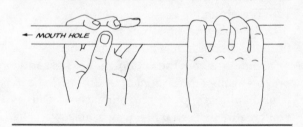

Figure 42

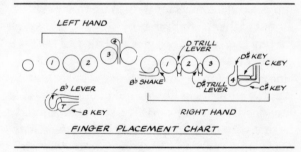

Figure 43

figure 43, the finger placement chart. (On this chart and those following, the thumb is represented by *T*; the remaining fingers of each hand are numbered 1 to 4, starting with the forefinger.) Make sure your left thumb is on the B key, not the B-flat.

38

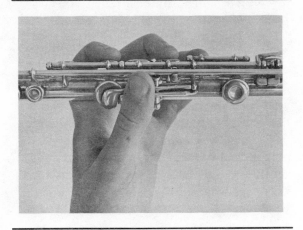

Figure 44

The entire left hand should be perpendicular to the flute, with the wrist bent backward. The side of the forefinger rests against the flute body, so that all the left hand fingers come onto their keys at a diagonal. The forefinger curls under the flute to form a supporting cradle.

The right wrist should be kept straight, so that the hand and forearm form a straight line; or it may be bent just slightly forward. The fingers approach the flute straight on, not at an angle as those of the left hand do. The thumb is placed directly under the forefinger.

This hand position is designed so that the flute can be entirely supported by three points: the cradle of the left forefinger, the right thumb,

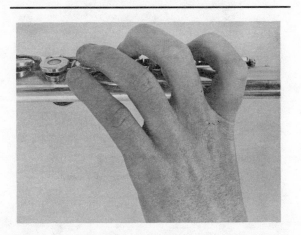

Figure 45

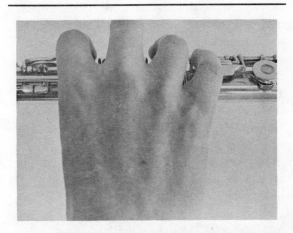

Figure 47

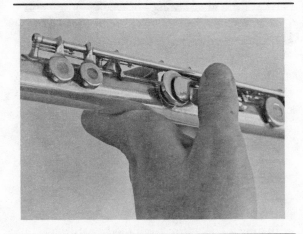

Figure 46

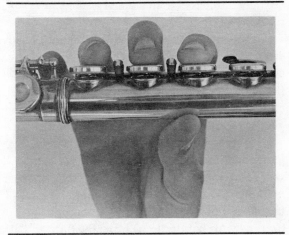

Figure 48

and the right little finger, which is kept pressing down its key for almost all notes. Most of the weight of the flute is divided about equally between the left forefinger and the right thumb; the little finger holds the flute steady from the top. This frees all other fingers to perform one function only: pressing and releasing the keys.

Practice holding the flute with these support points, and all other fingers off the flute. This may give you some trouble at first, but your hands will gradually adjust.

All fingers (except the thumbs) should be slightly arched, so that they approach their keys at about a 45-degree angle, with the fingertips hitting in the exact centers of the keys. (This is especially important on an open-hole flute, where the fingertips have to seal off the center holes.) On the closed-hole flute, all the fingers may rest lightly on their keys (taking care not to inadvertently press any of them partway down); or the ring, middle, and forefinger of each hand can be held a fraction of an inch above the keys, at equal height. On the open-hole flute, you *must* keep these fingers above their keys—otherwise you are making it a closed-hole flute and losing the advantages of open-holed keys. In all cases, the little fingers and left thumb should remain in contact with their keys.

At this point you are ready to adjust the flute assembly individually to yourself. To adjust the foot joint, place all your right-hand fingers on their keys, and hold that hand at perfect right angles to the flute. Now rotate the foot joint so that your little finger can easily reach and press any key of the foot joint *without moving the rest of the hand.*

For the head joint adjustment, hold your head straight up, and the flute pointed directly to the side, so that they are at right angles. Balance the flute on the three basic support points, and blow the note. Rotate the head joint until you get the clearest, loudest, most solid sound.

Remember both the head joint and the foot joint positions, and assemble your flute in that way from now on. (Some flute head joints have markings to help you.) You may find you have to change the positions slightly from time to time, as your hands "grow into" the flute and as you become more sensitive to the requirements

of your instrument. At these times, you may suffer a temporary loss of facility and tone.

Head and Arms

To find the correct position for your head and the flute, start with your head held straight up, and the flute held straight to the side. Now, keeping your head perpendicular to the flute, move the far end of the flute slightly forward and down; this means your head will have to rotate to the left and tilt

Figure 49

to the right. *Do not bend your head forward.* This would seriously constrict your air flow, and that is one of the major causes of weak volume and tone among beginners. Also, your bottom lip should not be used as a support for the flute. It must remain loose (on the metal flute) to maintain flexibility of expression and to keep the lips from tiring quickly. The three points described earlier should be sufficient to support the flute.

The elbows are held comfortably, just slightly away from the body, neither drawn in nor raised to the sides. (If lifting your elbows high seems necessary for fingering, then either your hand position or your flute assembly needs adjusting.) The entire combined posture of arms, head, and flute, is designed to require the least possible effort, while not creating any serious restrictions to the flow of the breath.

Torso and Legs

The back should always be held absolutely straight, with the shoulders comfortably back. This opens up the chest, thereby increasing the air capacity; it also gives maximum freedom of movement to the diaphragm, resulting in greater control of the flow of breath. A bent-over posture is another major cause of weak playing among beginners.

For the sake of free diaphragm movement, a standing position is by far the best. Both feet should be firmly planted, with your weight distributed equally between them. They can be placed in whatever way you feel most comfortable—together, spread, one foot slightly forward, etc. If you choose to sit instead, the thighs should be pointed as far downward as possible. You can do this by sitting on the edge of a chair, and tucking your legs under.

Other Aspects

Relaxation. Your entire body should be thoroughly relaxed. Tension can "freeze you up" by cutting down on your breathing flexibility and on your ease of movement in both the fingers and the embouchure. It also stops up your musical creativity. A relaxed body, on the other hand, allows the free flow of the music to the flute. Particular areas to be aware of are the abdomen, the shoulders, the throat, and the face.

Relaxing the body, of course, may involve examining and dealing with the source of the tension. Often this will come from an intense need you feel to play at a certain level of skill, or to gain the approval of others for your performance. In this case, it may be helpful to consider the idea that the most important part of flute playing is the *enjoyment* you get out of it—not any results measured in terms of "achievement," or anyone else's opinion of what you're doing. The only thing that *needs* to happen in flute playing is for you to get the satisfaction of the playing itself.

Health. In chapter 4 we noted that even a slight deterioration of the instrument will create conditions that hinder your playing. Your body can also be thought of as an instrument, and the same principle applies: Your health will definitely be reflected in the quality of your playing. As a serious flutist, then, you will take care to maintain your body in as healthy a condition as possible.

Practicing Posture

Proper posture is not a technique that you master immediately; it is something that develops over a period of time. It is important to use correct posture whenever you play, so that after a while it works into your body and becomes a habit.

Playing in front of a mirror is one of the best tactics for a flutist, because you can constantly check your posture to make sure you're not drifting into bad habits. The Posture Checklist below can be copied and taped to the mirror, to serve as a handy check.

Posture Checklist

1. Weight on both feet
2. Body held straight
3. Shoulders and abdomen relaxed
4. Flute tilted *slightly* down and forward
5. Head perpendicular to flute
6. Head *not* bent forward
7. Elbows hanging naturally
8. Left hand perpendicular to flute
9. Right hand fingers approaching flute at right angles
10. Flute balanced on three points
11. Right thumb under forefinger
12. Fingers arched, hitting keys in their centers
13. Fingers resting on keys or held just above at equal height
14. Little fingers and left thumb resting on keys at all times
15. Face and throat relaxed

7
Playing Notes

Fingering and Blowing Principles

First octave. To produce the first set of notes on the flute—the "first octave"—the holes are closed in a row from the top (the end with the mouth hole). This is accomplished either directly by the keys that are pressed or by hookups between those and other keys. The farther the distance between the mouth hole and the first open hole, the lower the note.

The following exercise will give you the feel of playing the first octave. Hold the flute as described in chapter 6, with all keys open. Blow a note, and, as you're blowing, press each finger down in turn—first the left forefinger, then the left thumb, and so on—keeping each one down as you press the next. (If you have an open-hole flute, make sure your fingertips completely seal the holes in the centers of the keys.) Skip the left little finger, which opens rather than closes a hole when it is pressed. (Some flutes, common in Eastern Europe, have the opposite arrangement—an open G-sharp key—as described in chapter 3.) When you get down to the right ring finger, press down that finger and lift the right little finger *at the same time.* Your last note will be with all fingers down except the little fingers.

As you press down more of the keys, you will have to make the following embouchure adjustments:

1. Make your lip opening larger, with the lips pressed together less tightly at the sides.
2. Blow more easily.

3. Direct the breath more downward.

Notice that *neither the head nor the flute is moved* as part of the adjustments.

Go down the flute as far as you can without losing the sound, then start again from the top.

Second octave. To produce the second octave, start with the last note you played in the exercise above. Now tighten your lips a little and blow harder. (This "doubles up" the vibrations in the flute, as explained in the appendix.) You should get a much higher note—the first note of the second octave.

To go higher, simply lift your fingers off the keys one at a time, starting with the right ring finger. (The right little finger presses down its key again as the ring finger is lifted.) The embouchure adjustments are the reverse of those for going lower, as follows:

1. Make your lip opening smaller, pressing the lips together more tightly at the sides.
2. Blow harder, from the diaphragm—harder, but not faster. In other words, you're pushing out the same *amount* of air, but it has to be forced through the smaller lip opening, which will take a little more pressure. (Being forced through the smaller lip opening automatically speeds up the air—just as a river speeds up its flow where the bed narrows.)
3. Direct the breath more horizontally.

Go up the flute lifting successive fingers until you lose the sound. Then return to the bottom and start over, trying to get to the note with all holes open. (Don't worry if you can't make it at this point.)

Third octave. The same progression of embouchure adjustments will lead you into the third octave, in which the vibrations triple for some notes, and quadruple for others. The fingerings for this octave, however, are much more complicated, because of "venting"— leaving keys open to help the vibrations in the flute form properly.

Fingerings

Figure 50, the finger placement chart, shows the keys to be pressed by each

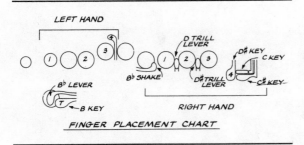

Figure 50

finger. The fingering chart in figure 51 gives all the standard fingerings for the modern flute, along with the letter name of each note and its musical notation. (A chart for flutes with open G-sharp keys is given in figure 125 in the appendix.)

Make sure your thumb is on the B key, not the B-flat lever. Notice that almost all the notes call for the right little finger to press the D-sharp key. Also notice that all fingers for the second octave are identical to those for the first, except the D and D-sharp.

To practice the fingerings, simply play down and up the chart. You may not be able to get to the lowest notes on the flute, as the keys on the foot joint are often out of adjustment. (See the section on regulation and leaky pads in chapter 4.) Try not to pause as you move from one octave into the next. Try to play at least as high as third octave D. Higher notes can be added as your technique improves and as the need arises. Memorize the fingerings as quickly as possible, so you can play all the notes without looking at the chart.

Articulation

The way notes are begun and ended is called *articulation.* The basic way of starting a note on the flute is to release the breath with the tip of the tongue, in a light "t" sound. When notes are played one right after the other, the beginning of each note becomes the end of the one previous. A note with no others following can be ended by lightly returning the tongue to the roof of the mouth, or simply by stopping the air flow.

A series of notes can also be played *legato* (smoothly) by giving a definite beginning only to the first note. Legato playing and normal articulation are generally alternated for variety.

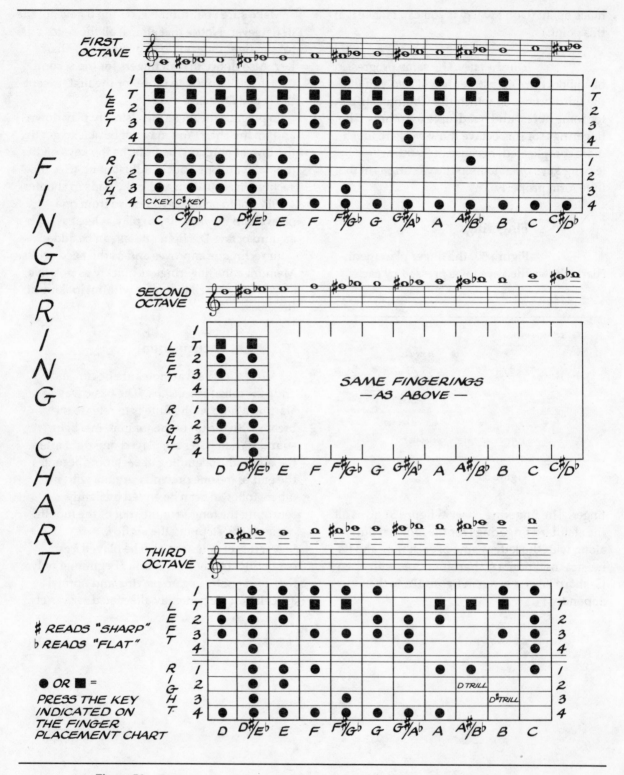

Figure 51

8

More about
Embouchure and Breath

Taking Breaths

In your playing, you should never come near to running out of breath, as this will make you lose control of the air flow. Full breaths should be taken whenever pauses in the music allow them. Practice inhaling quickly (and quietly) through your mouth and nose simultaneously.

Intonation

Intonation refers to the tuning of the individual notes of the flute to each other, as accomplished by embouchure adjustments. These notes are seldom exactly in tune by themselves, partly due to a small amount of mistuning that is unavoidably built into the flute and partly due to some of the dynamics of music making. It is constantly necessary, then, to "bend" individual notes slightly lower (flat) or higher (sharp).

To bend a note flat, blow more downward; to bend it sharp, blow more horizontally. This adjustment is made by moving the *lips only*— not your head or the flute. The movements are very slight. If you listen to the tuning of the notes you're playing, you'll find that the adjustment soon becomes automatic.

Volume Adjustments

If you try to play a note louder or softer just by changing how hard you blow the note will go out of tune. Instead, the following adjustments are used:

To play louder, blow faster and at the same time enlarge the lip opening. To play more softly, blow more slowly and make the lip opening smaller. (These adjustments will keep the breath speed constant, while changing the amount of air that hits the blowing edge.)

Developing Tone

There is no one flute tone—many different types of sounds can be produced on the instrument. Generally, you should attempt to make the kind of sound you like to hear. Though there are some guidelines for experimentation on this (some will be given in chapter 11), the best advice that can be given is to "think the sound": you will tend to produce the sound that is in your mind. As an aid in developing your conception, it is helpful to listen to flutists whose sound you admire, either live or on recordings.*

---

*My own favorite recordings for this purpose are those of Hubert Laws on the CTI label.

You may run into various problems in trying to develop a pleasing tone. A common one is breathiness. Some sound of the breath may be unavoidable, but most of it comes from inefficient blowing—breath that misses the blowing edge. You can check the focus of your own blowing by cleaning the lip plate and then seeing where the moisture from your breath condenses.

Breath may miss the edge because your lip opening is not centered properly in relation to the flute's mouth hole. Remember, this lip opening must be centered whether or not it's in the center of your mouth. Another possibility is that your lip opening is wider than the blowing edge, so that breath gets lost to the sides. Too round or too narrow a lip opening can also cause breathiness. Variations in your individual mouth structure may require you to make special adjustments.

A tone that sounds small and thin generally means that too much of the mouth hole is being covered by the lower lip, or that the head joint is turned too far inward, or that you are bending your head forward. A "hollow" tone can be caused by not enough of the mouth hole being covered or by the head joint being turned too far away from you; this will also cause problems in producing the higher octaves and require greater amounts of air for blowing.

Shrillness on the high notes can usually be reduced by pushing your lips a little more forward for those notes.

Exercises

Long tones. An excellent exercise for the development of both tone and breath control is called "long tones." It is exactly what it sounds like—you take a full breath and hold one note at a moderate volume for as long as you can (without losing control at the end). Repeat this for all notes within your range.

Listen carefully to the *quality* of each note. Work toward making it rock-steady—with no wavering at all, in either volume or tuning. The type of breathing required has been compared to the rotation of a planet around the sun—it is forever falling, forever pulling away, in perfect equilibrium. Also work toward making the tone as clear as possible.

This is not an easy exercise and not one you should expect to master immediately! Advanced players as well as beginners use it, because it builds the foundations of all good embouchure and breathing techniques.

Louder, softer. A variation on the long tones exercise can be used to practice adjustments for volume. As you're holding the note, make it gradually louder, then softer, all the while keeping it exactly in tune.

Octave jumps. On each fingering, jump rapidly back and forth between the first two octaves, articulating each note. This is excellent for developing embouchure flexibility and accuracy.

9
Fingering Technique

Difficult Combinations

As a beginning flutist, you will come across many sequences of notes, or *combinations,* that are at first difficult to finger. As a general rule, you should pause whenever you find one, and practice it—or at least remember it and come back to it later. Consistently ignoring them can only lead to deep-seated problems in your technique. On the other hand, if you master difficult combinations when they arise, they'll no longer be difficult!

Combinations can be difficult for various reasons. A particular finger (such as a little finger) might be weak; in this case, exercise it simply by having it open and close its key for a while. Many beginners have trouble moving particular fingers independently of others. If you have this problem, practice having such a finger open and close its key while watching to make sure no other finger is moving. The ring fingers commonly have this problem.

Sometimes a combination will be confusing because of the particular mixture of keys that are to be lifted and depressed; many transitions between octaves are difficult for this reason. On others, you might have trouble coordinating two specific finger movements, especially if they are going in opposite directions—as in the transition between D and E, in which the right ring finger and the little finger move in opposite ways. In all such cases, the fingers must move *at the same instant*—neither finger should be allowed to move before the other.

Runs

A *run* is a patterned sequence of notes that is played up and down the flute, at various speeds. (Scales are a common example.) Runs can be useful in developing evenness, facility, and speed of fingering; in coordinating the embouchure adjustments with the fingers; and in grouping notes that commonly go together in music in the player's mind. Some runs can also be used directly in improvisation.

In terms of fingering technique, the primary focus of practicing runs should be on developing evenness, not speed. (Speed will later grow out of evenness.) For this reason, steady timing is essential. Most flutists will find that a metronome is very useful for this. (Either a manual or an electric metronome can be used, but a manual metronome at its slowest speed should not be counted on for accuracy.)

Runs should be played from the lowest to the highest notes you can play—or vice versa—in one continuous motion, without halting or hesitation. Where possible, the run should be practiced in both directions, without any break when the direction is changed. If you find you are hesitating at any point—such as a change of direction or in a transition between octaves—practice that spot separately, or slow down the entire run until you can do it evenly.

When you are first practicing a run, it's a good idea to start at a moderate speed—one at which you can easily control the action—and work to make it gradually *slower* from there; then, in a second phase, make it progressively faster.

Working more slowly at first lets you gain thorough control of the muscles, so that the run becomes much easier to master at the faster speeds.

The most common runs used as exercises are the *scales*. These are groups of notes that normally form the basis for a piece of music. Practicing scales, then, not only is valuable for developing fingering technique but also helps you get used to commonly used groupings. (For a full listing of scales, and a further explanation of them, see chapter 13.) Like all other runs, the scales should be played through all the octaves in one continuous motion. They should be memorized as quickly as possible, so that you can play them without worrying about the notes.

Another type of run commonly used as an exercise is the *arpeggio*. Arpeggios are formed by separating chords into a series of single notes and playing them up and down the octaves. Since chords, like scales, are basic building blocks of music, this exercise too can familiarize you with common note groupings. (Further explanation and a listing of chords are given in chapter 13.) Again, you should memorize the notes as quickly as possible.

You can develop other runs for yourself, or pick them up from the playing of other musicians. Here are some illustrative possibilities:

1. Play all the notes, up and down the octaves. (All the notes together are referred to as the *chromatic scale*.)

2. On the major or minor scales, play two notes going up, then one down, then two up, then one down, etc.

3. Do the same exercise on the chromatic scale.

4. Starting high on the flute, play one note up, then two going down, again one up, and two down, on the major, minor, or chromatic scales.

5. On the chromatic scale, play the first note, then the fourth note up, then the fourth note down; move up the scale one note and repeat. (Sample segment: C, E, C, C-sharp, F, C-sharp, D, etc.) Reverse.

6. On the major and minor scales, play the first note, then the seventh note up, then the sixth down, then the seventh up from that note, the sixth down, etc. Reverse.

10
Tuning

Tuning means raising or lowering all the notes of an instrument so that they match either the notes of another instrument, or a certain "standard." On the flute, the notes are raised or lowered by moving the head joint in or out.

Concert Pitch

Today's flutes are constructed to play at *concert pitch*—the international standard—when the head joint is pulled out ⅛ inch (3 millimeters). (In France, concert pitch is set slightly below the international standard.) This measurement may vary slightly with differences in the mouth structure of the individual player or even with room temperature, so your flute may have to be adjusted when you are playing in groups. For solo playing, exact concert pitch is not required.

The flute will have its best internal tuning when tuned close to concert pitch; the farther the head joint is moved, the more the notes of the flute will be out of tune with each other.* This will cause your lips to tire more quickly from the increased "bending" needed to bring the notes into tune; the tone may also suffer. For these reasons, it's best if you can stay close to concert pitch. (Of course, this may not always be possible when playing with other musicians or with recordings.†)

Tuning with Others

When playing with others, some tuning is nearly always necessary. Before you tune, warm the flute by closing all the keys and blowing directly into the mouth hole for about a minute (somewhat longer for a wooden flute). This is to anticipate the rise in pitch that would otherwise occur when you begin playing.

The best note to use for tuning is first octave A, which is exact in terms of the internal tuning of the flute. Play the note at a moderate volume—loud or soft blowing may throw off its tuning. The tuning can also be thrown off by bending your head over the flute, having the flute's head joint rotated (toward you) too far, or pressing your bottom lip too hard on the lip plate.

When you are tuning with another musician, it is best to play your note first; otherwise you may have a tendency to "bend" your note to match the other (Between two wind instruments, of course, the order doesn't matter.) Listen carefully to whether your note is higher or lower—sharp or flat. To raise the pitch of your flute, push the head joint farther in; to lower the pitch, pull the head joint out (see figure 52). *Do not move the head joint cork to tune the flute.* (See the section on this cork in chapter 4.) Be careful to return the mouth hole to its

---

*On a revised scale flute (see chapter 3), the internal tuning will be best when the flute is tuned *exactly* to concert pitch. Other flutes—meaning nearly all flutes as of this writing—will play better when tuned slightly flat (assuming the head joint cork is left in standard position).

---

†If you find that your recordings are consistently tuned away from concert pitch, your turntable or tape player may be slightly off speed, and you should have this checked and adjusted. If you happen to be in the market for high-quality stereo equipment, it is a good idea to buy a turntable or tape player with a variable speed control, so that you can tune the recordings to concert pitch.

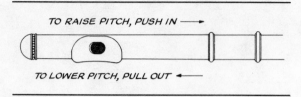

TO RAISE PITCH, PUSH IN ⟶

TO LOWER PITCH, PULL OUT ⟵

Figure 52

previous alignment with the rest of the flute, before checking the tuning.

When you are playing with a guitar or other instrument that does not have the pitch "built in," it is usually best to have the other musician tune to your flute, so that you can play near concert pitch.

If you don't have a chance to do a formal tuning—for instance, if you're playing with a record—you just have to play along at first and gauge your tuning as best you can, trying not to bend your notes as you gauge it. Adjust your

tuning from a sample, and then start again.

The flute has a fairly wide tuning range. If you can't push the head joint far enough in, pull it out and play with a different set of notes. If you can't pull it out enough, push it in and do the same.

A common problem among beginners is not realizing that the flute is out of tune. They may compensate by bending notes or making improper adjustments of their posture. Or the flute itself may be in tune, but the player's posture may be throwing the tuning off. Again, increased note-bending is required to compensate. If your lips are tiring quickly, and your highest and lowest notes are particularly hard to produce, first make sure you're not pressing your bottom lip down too hard, or bending over the flute. Next, rotate the flute until you find the proper angle, where the tone is strongest and loudest. If your tuning is off at that point, move the head joint.

11
Advanced Techniques

The techniques described in this chapter are advanced in the sense that they build on or supplement previously learned skills. In general, it is best that you put off working with them until you have made some progress with the techniques described in previous chapters.

Vibrato

Vibrato is the pulsing sound that you commonly hear used by singers, wind instrument players, organists, and others. It is one of the most important devices available to the flutist to make the music "come alive."

Vibrato is created by a series of "pushes" by the diaphragm. To get the feel of the diaphragm control required, jerk in your stomach a few times in quick succession, feeling the breath rush out of your mouth each time—in other words, do a belly laugh. Now do the same thing while blowing a note on the flute. That should give you your first vibrato.

It will probably take a while for you to develop the control necessary for a good vibrato. Start by working with a fairly slow pulsing—as slow as necessary to maintain a steady rhythm. The pulsing should be smooth (not like the "belly laugh"). As your diaphragm control develops, gradually work up to faster and faster speeds. A metronome may be helpful in developing steadiness.

Many beginners have a tendency to produce a vibrato with the throat muscles. This should be carefully avoided, since throat vibrato is generally impossible to control in speed and is too fast and "staccato" for normal Western music. (Throat vibrato should not be confused with the feeling of the pulses in the throat that accompanies diaphragm vibrato.)

The vibrato effect comes from fluctuations in volume, pitch, and tone quality of the note—all occurring at the same time. When the diaphragm pushes, the volume is at its loudest, the note is in tune, and the tone is "brilliant"—this is the "note" that the listener hears. When the diaphragm relaxes, the volume drops off, the note goes flat, and the tone becomes "dull"—this gives the effect of the pulse.

Playing vibrato has two interesting side effects for the player. Since for a good part of the time the note is not being blown at full volume, much less breath is required. Also, it is easier to hold a note in tune when it is being played vibrato.

The main use of vibrato is on long notes, to "enliven" them. It can also be used in any number of other places, which you will discover by listening and experimenting. You will also learn to vary the speed and intensity of your vibrato for maximum effectiveness. It's important to remember, however, that a constant use of vibrato can become as tedious as its complete absence.

Tonal Variation

A great deal of tonal variation is possible on the flute. A previous chapter advised you to "think the sound" in order to develop your basic tone. The same advice can be given to help you develop varieties of tones for use in your playing. Of course, you need to be familiar with various tones, from your listening and/or experimenting, to have a stock of sounds on which to draw. Here are some guidelines for experimentation.

A "richer" tone can be produced in the following way:

1. Thin the embouchure opening—make it into more of a slit than an oval—by drawing back the corners of the mouth.

2. Pull back the lips.

3. Blow a little harder.

To get a "purer" tone, do the opposite of the above.

Another way to approach tonal variation is through vowel sounds. Place your mouth in the shape it would take to pronounce one of the various pronunciations of the vowels—a, e, i, o, u—and play the flute while retaining that shape. ("E" gives the richest tone, "u" the purest.)

Alternative Fingerings, Trills, Tremolos

Alternative fingerings can sometimes be used to facilitate rapid and/or complex combinations of notes. They can be especially useful for trills and tremolos—rapid alternations between notes. (*Trill* refers to an alternation of two notes that are a half or whole step away from each other; *tremolo* refers to an alternation of notes farther apart.) In general, the tone and tuning of the alternative fingerings are not as good as those of the standard fingerings. For this reason they should be used only when necessary and only when the note will be passed over quickly.

Note: *It is not a good idea to try to learn the following fingerings until you are completely familiar and comfortable with the standard fingerings.* Otherwise, extreme confusion could result!

Some alternative fingerings are built into the key mechanism of the flute itself. A commonly used one is the alternative F-sharp (figure 53). Another is the B-flat lever. (See figure 54, the finger placement chart, for this and other keys

mentioned here.) In pieces of music in which B-flat is consistently played instead of B, this can be used as the key for the left thumb to rest on and press.

There are several keys built into the flute just for the playing of trills. The B-flat shake can be used to trill between B and B-flat (see figure 55). (This makes three ways to get B-flat on the flute.) The D trill lever can be used to trill between C or C-sharp and D (see figure 56); it is also extremely useful at any other time the player must pass rapidly from C or C-sharp up to D and back again. The D-sharp trill lever can be used similarly, between C-sharp and D-sharp (see figure 57).

Often, in rapid fingering, a key that you would normally move can be left up or down. In a quick playing of the second octave D, for instance, you could leave the left forefinger down (see figure 58). Rapid fingering in the

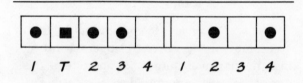

Figure 53

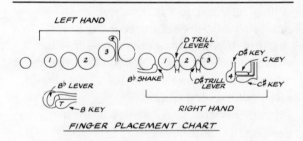

FINGER PLACEMENT CHART

Figure 54

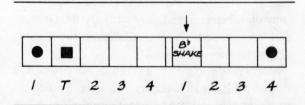

Figure 55

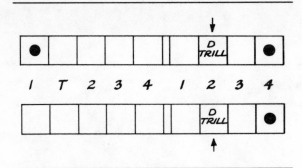

Figure 56

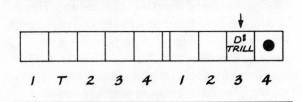

Figure 57

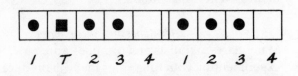

Figure 58

bottom of the second octave may make it necessary to leave the D-sharp key unpressed for several notes.

This type of altered fingering is often used for trills and tremolos. An example is the trill between B-flat and C (see figure 59). Another is the tremolo between G-sharp and B (see figure 60). Third octave trills and tremolos have many such possibilities.

You can experiment and find your own alternative fingerings as the need arises.

Multiple-Tonguing

On rapid successions of articulated notes, you may be unable to keep up with the music if you use the standard "t" articulation. A faster form of articulation is called *double-tonguing*. You rapidly alternate between a "t" and a "k"—t-k, t-k, etc. (Some players have an easier time with "d" and "g" or some other combination.) Each note must sound closely enough like the others so that the listener will not be able to tell that double-tonguing is being used. To practice double-tonguing, start at a slow speed, at which you can perfectly balance the strength of the two consonants; then gradually work faster, being careful not to sacrifice evenness as you gain speed.

For still faster articulation, or for triplets (notes grouped in threes), triple-tonguing can be used: t-k-t, t-k-t, etc. The same principle of evenness applies here.

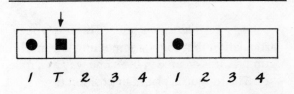

Figure 59

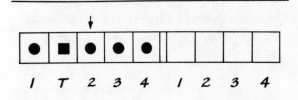

Figure 60

12
Special Effects

Special effects—used in moderation—can be valuable in adding spice to your playing. This chapter presents some of the possibilities available to the flutist, both on the instrument itself, and through the use of electronic devices. Don't limit yourself to this list—experiment and invent your own sounds!

Acoustic Effects

Consonants. Experiment with using other consonants besides "t" for articulation.

Flutter-tonguing. This is a type of articulation that sounds something like machine gun fire. It is created in the same way as a rolled "r": The tongue is placed in position to articulate "tr" or "dr," and the sides of the tongue are curled up to close off the air passage. (If you can't curl your tongue, you're out of luck!) The breath is then forced through at a pressure that will flutter the tip of the tongue. Flutter-tonguing is easiest on the higher octaves.

Fade-out. A complete fade-out can be achieved by getting gradually softer but continuing to blow even after the note has stopped sounding.

Note-bending. Previously, note-bending has been discussed in relation to bringing notes into tune, but it can also be used to shift notes *out* of tune. You can start a note in tune and bend it flat or sharp; or you can start it flat or sharp and bend it back into tune. This effect has become popular with the influence of the blues and of Eastern musical forms on Western music.

Normally, the large shift discussed here is accomplished by rotating the flute and/or leaning the head forward or back. On the open-hole flute, it can also be produced by shifting a finger on or off the hole in the center of a depressed key (half-holing).

Quarter-tones and micro-tones. Many classical flutists and composers are now experimenting with fingerings that will produce notes between the notes of our Western chromatic scale. Some fingering guides for this are now becoming available.

Multiphonics. Another area of current experimentation among classical flutists is multiphonics. By careful blowing, a player can find a space "between" two octaves, in which two notes can be heard simultaneously. Fingerings are being developed to facilitate this.

Singing into the flute. As you're playing, sing the syllable "doo" into the flute—that's right, with your voice! The effect is a sort of buzzing, along with the sound of the flute. (This effect was popularized first by Roland Kirk and later by Ian Anderson of the rock group Jethro Tull.)

Blowing through the octaves. As you're playing a trill or tremolo, change your

54

embouchure and breath pressure to shift rapidly up through the higher octaves, then down again.

Underblowing ("whistle stops"). Hold your embouchure as if playing the second octave, and blow very softly—so softly that the flute body doesn't even sound. What you will hear is a series of very small whistlelike tones, something like pipes playing in the far distance. This can be amplified for performance.

Key "clicks." Take the fingering of any first-octave note, and slap down the final key to be closed (without blowing). You will hear a soft, short musical tone. It is actually possible to play melodies in this way. This is another effect that can be amplified.

Electronic Effects

General. Any of the electronic devices originally intended for the electric guitar can be used by the flutist: tone controls, vibrato control, wah-wah pedal, fuzz-tone, etc.

Reverb. Reverb gives the effect of playing in a large building with a lot of echo; it is a favorite among flutists. Reverb controls are built into most amplifiers and PA systems; if not, they can be obtained as separate devices.

Tape-loop. The tape-loop machine is a tape recorder that records and plays back simultaneously on a continuous loop of tape. In this way the flutist can build up "layers" of sound, giving the effect of a number of interweaving flute parts. The trick is to coordinate your playing with the cycle of the loop (this is adjustable on the machine).

Octave divider. This device takes the note you're playing, changes it into another octave, then sends it through the speaker at the same time your own note is coming through. It sounds as if you were playing in two octaves at once.

Synthesizer. Woodwind musicians can now "play" a synthesizer with the notes of their instruments, in much the same way that keyboards have previously been used. The device that makes this possible is called a synthesizer *interface.** Use of the interface requires a pickup with a minimum of "key noise."

---

*A current United States manufacturer is 360 Systems, Los Angeles, California.

Part IV

Making Music

13

Scales and Chords

Whether you intend to read music or to play by ear, it will be valuable for you to understand about two of the basic building blocks of Western music—scales and chords.

Scales

A scale is a series of notes from which the notes of a piece of music are drawn. The two most important types of scales used in Western music are the major scale and the minor scale.

The major scale is familiar to almost everyone as do, re, mi, fa, sol, la, ti, do. A scale is named after the note that is used as "do"—so a major scale starting on C would be a *C major scale*, or *C scale*, for short. (If it was a C *minor* scale, you would *have* to say "minor.") You can find the major scale of any note by starting with that note, singing the do, re, mi, and picking out each note on the flute.

You can also find the scale by measuring it out. This is done by moving up after each note either a *half-step* (one note) or a *whole step* (two notes). After do, you move up a whole step to come to re. Mi is another whole step up, then fa is a half-step above that; and so on. The complete pattern is shown in figure 61.

There are actually several types of minor scales, but the most common is the *natural* minor. In this scale, mi, la, and ti are all moved down a half-step, from their major scale positions. (In other common types of minor scales, either la or ti is *not* moved down.) The complete pattern of this scale is also shown in figure 61.

Another way to find the notes of a minor scale is to count up three half-steps from do and play the major scale of that note—the minor scale of your original do will have the exact same notes. For instance, the scale of A minor has the same notes as a C major scale. (The lower scale is referred to as the *relative minor* of the higher, major scale.)

Figure 62, the scale chart at the end of this chapter, gives the written notation of all major and natural minor scales. Only one octave (the distance between do and do) is shown for each scale, but the scale continues with the same notes up and down the flute. The second and third lines in figure 62 (C-sharp major/A-sharp minor and D-flat major/B-flat minor) are two notations for the same notes. In the rest of the scales and key signatures, only one notation is given for each (E-flat major, for example), although the name of the other scale (D-sharp major, in that example) is also given. (The "key signature" column will be explained in chapter 15.)

How are these scales used in music? Most songs are based entirely on the notes of only one scale; almost all others use one scale as a

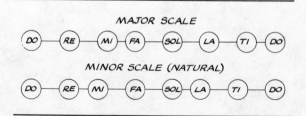

Figure 61

foundation, switch to other scales, and then return. The main scale used in a piece is called the *key* of the piece. For example, if a piece of music uses the C major scale entirely or mostly, then it is said to be in the *key of C major* (or just the *key of C*).

Once you know the key of a piece of music, you know all or most of the notes that you will be working with. This simplifies your playing a good deal, especially when you have become thoroughly familiar with the various scales. Doing scales as an exercise (as suggested in chapter 9) can help you to gain this familiarity.

Major and minor scales are the predominant ways of grouping notes in Western music, but they are certainly not the only ways it can be done. The ancient Greeks used seven different diatonic (seven-note) scales, from which our own scales are selected. (The eighth note—the high "do"—is not counted, because it is considered the first note of the next octave.) All seven of these scales can still be found in Appalachian and British folk music. The music of southern India recognizes seventy-two different diatonic scales!

Some modern Western composers have used a scale of twelve notes in an octave (the *chromatic scale*)—in other words, all the notes on the flute. Recent experimenters have built special instruments to play scales of thirty-nine tones per octave and more. Meanwhile, large portions of the world rely almost completely on a five-note *(pentatonic)* scale.

Chords

A *chord* is a group of several notes that together provide a structure for the notes of a piece of music to fit into. Almost any piece in Western music can be thought of as based on a series, or *progression* of chords. The notes of the chord can be played all together on one instrument—such as a piano or guitar—or, as is usual in classical music, by several instruments together, each playing one note. (In some cases, notes are "understood," rather than actually played.)

The simplest and most common form of chord is made up of three notes—the first, third, and fifth notes of a scale (do, mi, and sol). These chords are named for the scales from which they are taken—a chord taken from a C major scale would be a *C major chord,* or a *C chord;* a chord taken from a D minor scale would be a *D minor chord.* Another common type of chord is the *seventh* chord, which starts with a major chord and adds the seventh note of the scale (ti), lowered one half-step.

The chord chart, figure 63 (placed after the scale chart, figure 62), shows the notes in all major, minor, and seventh chords. Although the names of two notations for the same chord notes are given (for example, C-sharp and D-flat), only one notation is given for each set of chords. (You may find it valuable to practice these in the form of arpeggios, as described in chapter 9.) Many more types of chords are also found in Western music, but we will not describe them in this book.

How are chords used, and how do they relate to scales? Most songs start and end with what is called the *tonic* chord—a chord based on the key of the piece. (For instance, a song in the key of C would have a C chord as its tonic.) When this chord is played, you can play any note from the scale of the key on the flute, but the notes in the chord will exert a "pull" that will cause you to put the most emphasis on those notes.

When a different chord is played, your main emphasis will switch to the notes of the new chord. As long as all the notes of this chord are found in the scale of the key, you will continue to use that scale. (The chords of F major and G seventh, for example, contain only notes found in a C major scale.) But if the chord contains notes *not* found in that scale, you will have to temporarily switch to a whole new scale in order to play along with it.

The statements just made about use of chords are meant as approximate guidelines only, to give you a general feel of what happens in Western music making. The variations are endless, and you should feel free to create your own!

Figure 62

CHORD CHART

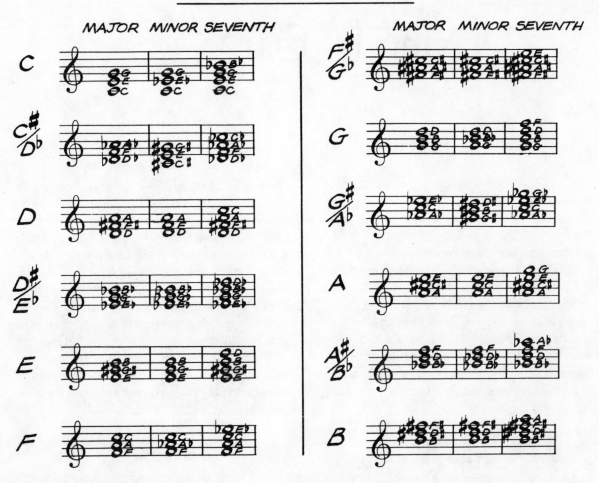

Figure 63

14
Playing by Ear

There's something very fine about having direct contact with music, without the intercession (or interruption) of a piece of paper. There is a feeling of greater personal involvement and also a greater freedom, because you are not relying on marks on paper to tell you what notes to play.

"Playing by ear" actually refers to two separate skills: copying (imitating) and improvising (creating). Since the ability to copy accurately is the technical foundation of improvisation, copying should generally be given the greater emphasis at first.

Copying

To start your practice in copying, choose simple songs—children's songs and folk songs are good—and pick out the notes to play them on the flute. (At first, try to start on notes that don't demand a large number of difficult fingerings.) Learn to play each song smoothly and easily. You can also try the same song starting on different notes. Gradually work into more difficult songs.

After a while, you may find it valuable to work with recorded music. Put on a song with which you are familiar, and learn to play along with the melody line. You might also try to copy other parts of the song—a chorus line, a bass line, or whatever other part appeals to you. The music with which you practice should be music you enjoy, because many of the note patterns (or *riffs*) you learn at this time will show up later in your improvisation.

Between any two successive notes in a song

there is a certain musical "distance," related to how many notes on the flute lie between them. A song is basically a series of these distances, or *intervals;* no matter where on the flute you start the song, the intervals will be the same, even though the notes are completely different. The real object of your practice in copying is to learn to *hear* these intervals—just as you learn to estimate inches or centimeters—and then to be able to play them anywhere on the flute.

Though copying may be difficult at first, you will find after a while that you can hear many songs and play them correctly the first time through.

Improvisation

In learning to improvise comes the joy of actually creating music. You are no longer restricted to the notes laid out for you by someone else; you can range into new territory, an explorer in your own right. Why limit yourself to music that has been meticulously formulated and preserved? An infinite store of music lies within each one of us, available to us at any moment, if only we will allow it to come out. Music is free!

Improvisation can be divided roughly into two basic types: *structured* and *free.* In structured improvisation, some type of framework is present—there is almost always a chord progression, generally a speed, a rhythm, sometimes an initial melody line with which to "lead off," possibly a distinctive bass line, an established order in which the improvising "soloists" are to play, etc. In free improvisation little or nothing is determined ahead of time, and the music develops almost entirely from the impulses felt by the musician or group.

Both types of improvisation can be done by either a single musician or a group. You can perform structured improvisation by yourself by "hearing" the chords in your head. You can do free improvisation in a group if the musicians are extremely sensitive to each other, but it becomes more difficult as the group becomes larger.

It's best to focus on structured improvisation first, since this will help you develop the resources you'll use in your free improvisation. Recorded music is excellent for practicing structured improvisation. After you've learned to copy various parts of a song, play along with it using your own notes. Hear which notes fit in at certain times, and which ones don't. What type of effect does the flute have to create to match the feel of the music, and how can you produce it? Will the music as a whole sound better if you "stay out" some of the time? Once you've worked this way for a while, you might try turning on the radio and playing with every song that comes on.

As soon as you feel fairly confident, get some musicians together and do the real thing! There are usually enough musicians around who are beginners on their own instruments so that you can find people who won't mind it if you make a few mistakes.

There is not a great deal I can tell you about learning free improvisation, because it's a fairly personal matter, but I will tell you two of my own favorite ways to do it. One is playing free improvisational duets with another flutist. The other is playing in a place with a lot of echo—an enclosed stairwell, a parking garage, a tunnel, a cathedral. Paul Horn, a well-known flutist, will actually travel to the other side of the world to try out an echo!*

In learning improvisation, it's valuable to be aware of the general "rules" of music making (as described in chapter 13), so that you can refer to them as needed; but it's not necessarily

---

*The resulting albums, *Inside* (recorded in the Taj Mahal), and *Paul Horn Inside the Great Pyramid,* are masterpieces of free solo improvisation.

helpful to apply them constantly in a conscious manner. Improvisation is learned largely by "feel," and focusing too much on the mechanics can actually slow down the learning process.

Help for the Tone-Deaf

Developing tone recognition. For many people, tone deafness is a stumbling block that prevents them from even *trying* to make music. Yet tone deafness isn't a built-in condition; it simply means that your ability to recognize tones has not yet been developed. There is a process that you can use to gain this ability.

Get a friend who can recognize tones to help you. Have the friend sing or play a particular note. Now, while the person is holding that note, try to match it by singing the same note. (The reason to start with singing is that it will help you internalize the feel of the note more quickly. If embarrassment prevents this, however, you can start by using the flute.)

If you matched it correctly, your friend will then pass on to another note. If you didn't, your friend will ask you if your note is higher or lower than the note you're trying to match. You'll say which you think it is, and then the friend will repeat the same note, and you'll try again. If yours was higher before, you'll now lower it; if it was lower, you'll raise it. Gradually you will learn to hear if it's higher or lower before you're asked, and you'll automatically adjust to match the note.

Once you've become accustomed to hearing higher and lower, you can continue the exercise on your own, using a piano, guitar, or any other instrument on which a note can be held. Hit random notes, and match your voice to them. You can check yourself on a tape recorder, if you have one available: Record yourself as you feel you're matching the note, then play back the tape. If you matched it, you'll hear only one note, otherwise two. Have someone check you occasionally to make sure you're doing it right.

The exercise will gradually become easier. When you feel you can match the notes with very little trouble, try the same exercise with your flute, starting again with help from your friend. (Before you do this, you should have the fingerings well memorized, so they won't get in the way. See chapter 7.)

The next step is to have your friend sing or play notes *without* holding them, and you match them from memory—first practicing with your voice, then with the flute. This exercise also can be continued on your own.

Finally, you can work at doing two notes in a row from memory, then three, four, etc. After a while you'll find that you can hear tunes in your head, and pick them out on the flute. And there you are! These exercises can, of course, be altered to meet your own needs.

Chord deafness. A problem related to tone deafness is what I call "chord deafness"—the inability to hear if a note "fits" in with a chord being played. This can be overcome with a similar approach to that described for tone deafness. Have a friend play a chord, sing a note that you think fits with the chord, and have your friend tell you if it does fit. After some practice with your friend, you can work by yourself, using another instrument or even a recording of chords. Finally, you can do the same exercises on the flute. As you gain the ability to quickly find a note that fits in, you can begin improvising with slow, simple music, and work up to faster music.

Though these processes require some patience, they do work, and they don't even take as long as you might imagine. So pick up that flute and make some music—you've run out of excuses!

15
Reading Music

The great benefit of learning to read music is that you make available to yourself a vast wealth of musical creativity handed down by the fertile minds of centuries of composers. It also opens up the possibility of musical fellowship with other individuals and groups that play written music. And it allows you to preserve and share musical compositions that you yourself develop, by putting them into written form.

Learning How

This chapter explains the Western method of music notation. It also gives hints on how to approach a piece of written music that you are trying to learn. Of course, actually learning to read music will happen as you work with the music itself. Beginners can start with elementary flute method books, or with simple song books. Your local music store may be able to recommend appropriate music literature.*

A valuable introduction to group playing can be provided by joining a recorder group. Music written for recorder is generally simple and well suited to the flute, and recorder groups will often welcome the addition of a flutist. Recorder groups and associations are quite common in many cities.

A music stand to hold the music you're reading will be a worthwhile investment. It is fairly inexpensive, and nothing else really can take its place.

_____
*Good flute pieces for beginners can be found in *Everybody's Favorite Flute Solos* (Amsco).

Staff and Clef

Western music notation is written on a pattern of five lines called a *staff* (see figure 64). A sign at the very beginning of the staff

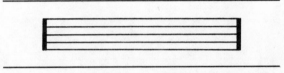

Figure 64

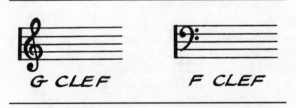

G CLEF   F CLEF

Figure 65

shows the range of notes represented on the staff. This is called the *clef* sign and the two in normal use are the *treble clef* (G clef) and the *bass clef* (F clef).* They are shown in figure 65.

Because all the notes of the (soprano) flute can be most easily shown on the treble clef, all flute music is written in that clef.

Each line and space of the staff represents the letter name of a note. Additional short lines are

_____
Clef is an Italian word, as are many of the other music terms you'll find throughout this chapter. Italian became the "universal" language of music several centuries ago, when Italian musicians were influential throughout Europe.

added above and below the staff as needed to represent higher and lower notes. Figure 66 shows the letter names of each line and space within the three-octave range of the flute.

Sharps (#) and flats (b) are notated by signs preceding the notes, as illustrated in figure 67.

Timing

While the position of the note on the staff determines which note it is, the type of note that is written determines the relative length of the note. Figure 68 presents the various types of notes. The *stem* of the note can be written up or down (see figure 69). Two or more notes with *tails* (the short wavy lines attached to the stems) are often *beamed* for aesthetic reasons (see figure 70).

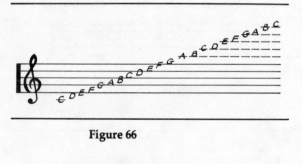

Figure 66

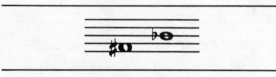

Figure 67

WHOLE NOTE   HALF NOTE   QUARTER NOTE   8TH NOTE   16TH NOTE   32ND NOTE   64TH NOTE

Figure 68

Figure 69

Figure 70

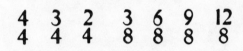

Figure 71

The time "value" of each of these types of notes is determined by the *time signature* at the beginning of the piece. This signature consists of two numbers. Commonly used time signatures are given in figure 71. The bottom number represents the type of note that is given one "count," or "beat." (One way to think of one count is that it equals a foot tap.) Usually this number is a four, representing a quarter note, or an eight, representing an eighth note. Once you know the type of note that gets one count, the values of all the other notes follow automatically. The chart in figure 72 shows time values for notes in the two most common arrangements.

A dot next to a note means it gets its normal number of counts plus half that number (see the examples in figure 73).

The top number of the time signature gives the number of counts in a *measure*. A measure is a rhythmic grouping of notes, usually distinguished by a recurrent pattern of *accents*—counts on which you would clap if you were clapping. Measures are divided by vertical lines (*bar lines*) on the staff (see figure 74). The most common numbers of counts in a measure are two, four, three, and six. Any other number is also possible—in jazz, for example, five or seven counts in a measure are not uncommon.

To read a time signature, then, look at the top number to find out the number of counts in each measure, and the bottom number to learn what type of note represents one count (see figure 75). The symbols in figure 76 are sometimes used in place of a regular time signature.

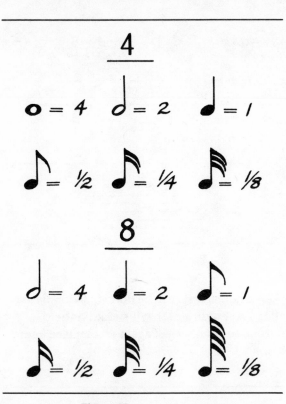

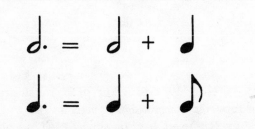

Figure 72

Figure 73

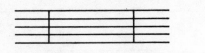

Figure 74

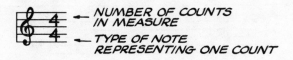
← NUMBER OF COUNTS IN MEASURE
← TYPE OF NOTE REPRESENTING ONE COUNT

Figure 75

$\mathbf{c} = \frac{4}{4}$ "COMMON TIME" $\mathbf{\not{c}} : = \frac{2}{2}$ "CUT TIME"

Figure 76

Key Signature and Accidentals

When a piece is written in a key with sharps or flats, instead of writing down a sharp or flat sign every time a note appears, a key signature is given at the beginning of the piece to show what notes will be sharped or flatted *throughout the piece* (unless otherwise notated). The signs are placed on the lines and spaces on which the notes to be sharped or flatted will appear. For instance, in the example in figure 77, F and C will be played as sharps.

Figure 77

In effect, this identifies the key in which the piece is written as either a particular major key or its relative minor. (The key signature in figure 77 indicates either D major or B minor.) For a full listing of key signatures and their corresponding scales, see the scales chart, figure 62, in chapter 13.

If a note within the piece is to be played differently from the way the key signature indicates, it must be individually notated. These notations are called *accidentals*. In addition to the usual sharp and flat signs, the signs shown in figure 78 are used.

An accidental applies both to the note on which it appears and to any reappearance of that note within the measure, unless otherwise notated. In the example in figure 79, the first F is played natural, both the second and the third Fs are played sharp, and the fourth is played natural again.

Figure 78

Figure 79

Figure 82

Key changes within the piece can be notated by a new key signature preceded by a double bar. This may also include instructions about notes previously sharped or flatted (see figure 80).

Like notes, rests can be dotted. A dot placed after a rest indicates that it should be held its normal count plus half again as long (see figure 83).

Figure 80

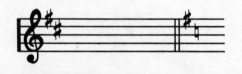

Figure 83

Rests

Counts during which the player does not play are indicated by *rests,* which are shown in figure 81. These rests have the time values of the notes after which they are named. The *whole rest,* however, is understood to have a time value of one measure, no matter what time signature is used. A rest meant to extend over a number of measures can be annotated as shown in figure 82, which indicates a rest of eight measures.

Repeats

When portions of the music are to be repeated, a *repeat sign* such as the one in figure 84 is used. If it appears by itself in a piece of music, it means the player is to repeat from the beginning. Otherwise, a specific part of the

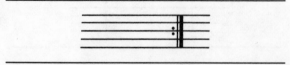

Figure 84

Figure 81

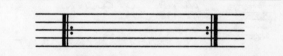

Figure 85

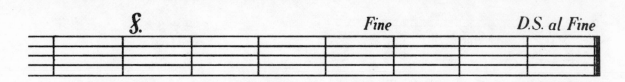

Figure 87

music that is to be repeated may be bracketed as shown in figure 85. The appearance of the arrangement in figure 86 shows that a different ending is to be played the second time through.

Repeats can also be indicated by the words *D.C. al fine,* meaning repeat from the beginning to the word *Fine,* or by the words *D.S. al fine,* meaning repeat from the sign to the word *Fine.* The sign is illustrated in figure 87. An instruction to repeat one previous measure may be written as shown in figure 88.

Figure 86

Figure 88

Volume and Dynamics

There are various ways of notating how the notes should be played.

A *slur* tying together two or more notes (see

Figure 89

figure 89) means that they should be played *legato* (smoothly), with only the first note articulated. The same sign appearing between two notes on the same line or space is called a *tie* (see figure 90) and indicates that they should be

Figure 90

Figure 91

played as one note, held for the length of time represented by both notes together.

A dot over or underneath a note (see figure 91) indicates that it should be played *staccato*—short and hard.

The following notations are used to indicate volume:

pp	pianissimo	very soft
p	piano	soft
mp	mezzo piano	moderately soft
mf	mezzo forte	moderately loud
f	forte	loud
ff	fortissimo	very loud

Figure 92 shows first a *crescendo*—a gradual increase in volume—then a *decrescendo* (or *diminuendo*)—a gradual decrease in volume. An

Figure 92

Figure 93

emphasis, or *accent,* on a particular note can be notated as shown in figure 93.

Tempo and Expression

Instructions for *tempo* (speed) and expressive quality are normally given at the beginning of the piece; often further instructions are given within the body of the music also. The following list contains the most common terms. Dictionaries of musical terms can be used for further reference.

accelerando	getting faster
adagio	slowly
ad libitum	same as *rubato*
allegro	fast
andante	moderate tempo, "walking tempo"
a tempo	in strict timing
con . . .	with . . .
dolce	softly and sweetly
largo	very slowly, grandly
lento	slowly
marcato	with emphasis
meno . . .	less . . .
moderato	moderately fast
molto . . .	very . . .
non tanto . . .	not too much . . .
non troppo . . .	not too much . . .
piu . . .	more . . .
presto	very fast
rallentando	getting slower
ritardando	getting slower
ritenuto	in a slower tempo, "held back"
rubato	not sticking to the strict time value of the notes
scherzando	playfully
sempre . . .	always . . .
sforzando	a sudden, strong accent
subito	suddenly
tenuto	held to the full time value of the note
vivace	lively

Miscellaneous Symbols

A *grace note* is a very short note tacked on just before another note. It is notated as shown in figure 94.

A *trill* is a rapid alternation between the note written and the next note up the scale. It is written as shown in figure 95.

A *triplet* is a group of three notes that is played in the time that would normally be taken for two notes. In the example in figure 96, the three eighth notes are to be played during one count.

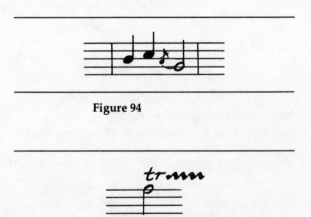

Figure 94

Figure 95

Figure 96

Figure 97

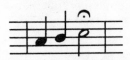

Figure 98

To reduce the need for writing a number of lines above the staff, the notation in figure 97 is often used, indicating that you are to play the notes one octave higher than written.

An instruction to hold a note an extra long time, and then pause, can be notated by a *fermata,* shown in figure 98.

Transposition

Flutes of sizes other than the soprano—alto, bass, E-flat, piccolo—are called *transposing* instruments. This means that, when you read music specifically written for these instruments, you use the same fingerings as would be indicated for a soprano flute, but the notes that actually come out are entirely different.

For example, if you played the note shown in figure 99 on a soprano flute, it would be a first octave C. If the same note appeared on music written for alto flute, you would use the same fingering as for the soprano, but the note would be a low G. All the written notes for these

instruments are treated in this way—by reading the *fingering,* rather than the actual note.

Transposition makes it possible for a flutist playing different sizes of flutes to learn only one set of fingerings in relation to written music. Of course, it thoroughly confuses the issue if the flutist also wants to read music that has *not* been transposed.

Learning a Piece of Music

Here are some suggestions about how to approach individual pieces of music. First try to sight-read (play without stopping) all the way through the piece, in order to get a general feel for it. Then come back and practice it a section at a time. A "section" could be four measures, or two, or eight—play however many you can best handle at a time. Sometimes these sections can be defined by rests in the music, or by the places where you take your breaths.

In each section, first, without actually playing for the moment, figure out everything that's happening with the notes and the rhythm. Tapping your foot on every count may be extremely helpful in working out complicated rhythms. Another aid is to follow the music with your eyes while verbally counting, "one and, two and, . . ."

When you have the section figured out, start practicing it at a slow enough tempo so that you do not make mistakes—no matter how slow that is! Start a few notes before the beginning of the section, and continue a few notes past it, so that you'll get used to the transitions between the parts you're practicing. As you feel more comfortable with the section, increase your speed, until you're playing it at normal tempo. Then move on to the next section.

When you have mastered each section separately, start from the beginning and play

Figure 99

through. Start at a slower tempo again, one at which you feel completely comfortable. If you make a mistake, stop and practice that portion, then back up a few measures and continue on. *Do not start again at the beginning*—this will result in your learning the beginning extremely well and the ending not so well at all. Increase the speed as you feel able, until you can play slightly *faster* than normal tempo. Then return to normal tempo, and you should have the piece pretty solidly.

Interpretation

It's important to remember that written music doesn't tell every detail of how the piece should be played. Rather, the notation and instructions provide a basic structure. "Filling out" the structure is left to the musician, who accomplishes this with all the tools of expressiveness. (Techniques of expressiveness are discussed in chapter 16.)

It is in interpretation of the music that the creativity of the musician comes through. If you listen to recordings of fine classical musicians playing the same piece of music, you will hear that no two of them play the piece exactly alike. In effect, the musician becomes a co-creator with the composer.

Nonclassical Music

The system of musical notation that we use was developed in the West specifically for classical music. It works very well for that music, but unfortunately not so well for folk, jazz, blues, or non-Western music. These styles tend to have many features for which there is no notation in our system— slides, "intermediate" notes, waverings, and many rhythmic "feels."

When reading transcriptions of these kinds of music, then, remember that there may be quite a bit that never got onto the page or that was written down incorrectly. The safest course is to develop a good feel for a particular type of music, by listening to it before trying to play from written music. It's also a good idea to memorize such pieces as soon as possible, to avoid the "dictatorship" of the notation.

16
Living Music

Playing music is more than just producing a series of notes. Whether you're creating your own music or playing another person's composition, it's up to you as flutist to breathe life into the music and make it come alive.

Expressive Techniques

Part of making music come alive is knowing and using the wide range of possibilities for variation that are available to you. (Some of the possibilities listed below apply more to improvisation than to other types of playing, while others are more widely applicable.)

Vary your volume within a long series of notes, or even on a single note. Use all three octaves, rather than allowing yourself to get stuck in one section of the flute's range. Use variations in tone, between pieces or within a piece.

Play notes in different ways. Use different types and strengths of articulation. Alternate articulated notes with legato playing. Vary the lengths of the notes.

Alternate between vibrato and "steady" blowing. Vary the speed and intensity of your vibrato.

In some situations you can be more or less free with your rhythm: starting notes slightly ahead of or behind the beat, interweaving with an established rhythm, or even playing in "free rhythm"—stretching and condensing notes as you like.

You can pick up other expressive techniques by listening to other musicians—and not just flutists, either! Vocalists, violinists, guitarists, and others can all suggest ways of expressing yourself on the flute. You will also discover many techniques on your own, often just by "thinking" of the type of effect you want to produce. The effect that is in your mind will tend to be produced on the flute—even if you didn't know you could make that sound! This is often expressed by the instruction, "Play as if you were singing."

One way of approaching expressiveness in music is through the concept of *phrasing*. This means that the music can be thought of and played as a series of note phrases, in much the same way as we speak in sentences. Each phrase has a definite beginning and end and conveys its own expressive "statement." Phrases are often defined by rests in the music, or by the places where you take a breath.

Phrasing helps to focus the listener's attention, which might be lost if the notes presented a long, uninterrupted flow (like a run-on sentence). Of course, the phrases themselves should be varied, in length and/or dynamics. (If you don't believe this, try asking someone ten questions in a row.)

In using expressive techniques, and in improvisation, it's important to remember that both repetition and variety are vital elements in music. The variety gives the music its life, but without some degree of repetition, the music becomes "scattered," without focus. Repetition supplies a framework, a point of reference, allowing the musician and the listeners to explore avenues of creativity without losing their bearings. The success of the music depends in part on the proper balance of these two elements.

Beyond Technique— Playing from Within

Almost everything we've discussed about playing the flute could be described as technique—the technique of playing the instrument, or the technique of making music. Good technique is the foundation of music making. You must work on it until it is an integral part of you, so natural that you don't have to think about it at all.

But at that point it becomes both possible and necessary for you to move beyond technique, because music is far more than that. The best music has a spark to it, a life of its own. You can tell when it's there—you can feel the energy. The spark makes all the difference between music that is living and music that's just a pleasant entertainment.

Where does that spark, that life, come from? It comes from deep within you. It cannot be produced by the hands, or even by the head. To find it, you must turn to a source far deeper than these—to the very center of your being.

Turn inward to that center, and open yourself completely to the impulses that flow out from it. Let them pour through you and out of you into the flute. Let yourself be an instrument, just as the flute is an instrument.

Then your music will truly live.

Part V

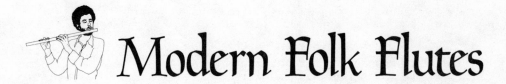

Modern Folk Flutes

17

Finding a Folk Flute

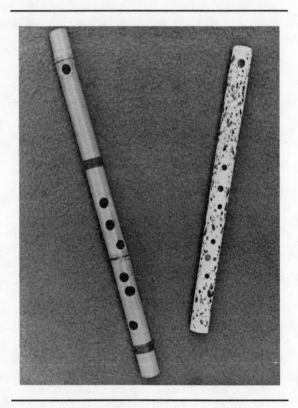

A whole new generation of folk flutes and flute makers is currently springing up in the Western world. At a time when our

Figure 100

society is becoming increasingly sophisticated and complex, these modern folk flutes are a return to simpler forms of the instrument that are found in other parts of the world and in our own past.

Why a Folk Flute?

Why would anyone want to play a folk flute when the modern classical flute is technically so far advanced? It's true that the classical flute is far superior in many respects, including the accuracy of its overall tuning, its consistency of tone and volume, fingering ease in all keys, and the ability to tune the entire instrument higher or lower. But folk flutes have their own unique advantages.

One very obvious one is price. The cost of even the cheapest classical flute is a substantial investment, while a well-tuned folk flute can be bought for $20 or less—well within the range of most players. (This price difference may make it worthwhile for you to start on a folk flute—to see if you enjoy playing—even if you eventually expect to play the classical flute.) Also, a classical flute requires professional servicing, and that cost can add up to a great deal over the life of the instrument.

Folk flutes are much more convenient to carry around than classical flutes. Most of them will stand up to rougher handling; they don't have to be assembled and taken apart; they can be taken to the beach (the sea air will corrode a metal flute or key mechanism); they take up little space in a backpack; and there is much less chance that they will be stolen.

With the wide variety of tones available in folk flutes, you might well come across a sound you actually prefer to that of the classical. Also, certain "sliding" and "bending" effects can be easily produced on the folk flute because of the direct finger contact with the holes, while these sounds are difficult or impossible to produce on the classical flute.

But probably the most important advantage of the folk flute over the classical is the "personal" quality of the flute. The direct use of the fingers on the holes, without the intervention of a complex key mechanism, makes it much easier for the player to experience a direct relation to the instrument and to the music being played. The way is made easy for you to join with the flute, to blend with it, to become one with it. This feeling of personal relationship is enhanced by the materials from which these flutes are most commonly made. Bamboo, wood, and clay have a personal warmth that cannot be approached by metal.

Finally, folk flutes are mostly made by hand, and by one person, who directs personal energy into each instrument by the flute-making process. The result is a product that speaks of humanness, of the relation between the maker, the material, the craft, and you, the player of the flute.

Where to Find Folk Flutes

The best places to buy a folk flute are at street stalls or craft shows, where you can have direct, personal contact with the maker. Folk flutes can also be found in some music stores, especially those that sell primarily to young people. These flutes might be made locally, or by one of a number of small companies that have begun distributing folk flutes throughout the United States.

Another way to get a flute is to order one through the mail, though this means you won't be able to select it personally. Addresses of flute makers selling by mail can be found in various spiritual and natural living magazines, which are generally available at natural food stores.

Side-Blown Flutes

Modern side-blown folk flutes are being made from many different materials, including bamboo, clay, wood, enameled copper, and plastic.* Bamboo—some of it native, but most of it grown commercially in Taiwan—is currently the most common. It is also one of the most "personal," since each piece is unique and requires slightly different working by the flute maker. These flutes are sturdy, unless subjected to sudden temperature or moisture extremes.

The enameling on many ceramic flutes is extremely beautiful. These flutes have a tendency to get broken, but they can be repaired with glue. Rosewood is currently a favorite among wooden flute makers. The accurate machining possible on wood, copper, and plastic flutes allows a closer tuning than is normally found on the more handmade instruments.

If you don't already know how to play a flute, ask the seller to help you select one, or bring along someone who plays. First explain what kind of flute sound you like—deep, high, or medium. When a flute is shown to you, ask to hear something played fast and something played slowly.

Many bamboo flutes are not tuned to any particular scale, and, if you just want to make some nice sounds, these may be fine for you. If you want to play songs, however, the tuning should be carefully checked (with the understanding that it isn't going to be perfect). Ask to hear all the main notes of the flute slowly, from bottom to top, and listen carefully for the *do, re, mi* of the scale. This will also let you hear the range of the flute: a well-designed folk flute will have at least two full octaves that can be played well.

If you are planning to play your flute with other people or with recorded music, then the flute should also be in standard pitch. This can be checked against a pitch pipe, tuning bar, etc. Flutes in the key of G are the most versatile for playing with various kinds of music; this is now the most common size being made in materials other than bamboo. (The irregularity of bamboo makes it impossible to standardize flutes in this

---

*I am personally distrustful of any flute made of or coated on the outside with synthetic materials, because they are likely to be toxic. For a further discussion of this, see my book *Flutecraft,* listed in reading list at the end of this book.

Figure 101

cover all the holes. (When trying this, use the proper hand position, described in chapter 19.) Some discomfort in reaching the holes is acceptable, since you can expect your hands to stretch a little as you continue to play. Finally, make sure that it's *your flute!*

Shakuhachi

In the strictest use of the word, a *shakuhachi* is the traditional Japanese form of flute (see chapter 1). In terms of Western folk flutes, however, it has come to mean any end-blown bamboo flute with an obliquely cut blowing edge. These range from instruments that are approximate copies of the Japanese model to flutes that bear very little resemblance to it.*

A shakuhachi that attempts to resemble the Japanese flute will have five finger holes—one of them a thumb hole—playing a *pentatonic* (five-note) scale. It consists of do, mi, fa, sol, and ti on the notes of a natural minor scale. (See chapter 13.) On a well-tuned flute, the note with all fingers off will be the same as the first

---

*On the west coast of North America, a number of flute makers have given their primary attention to the shakuhachi, in an attempt to make an instrument as true to the Japanese flute as possible. The craft of these makers has been developing impressively for several years now, and the area may someday produce a tradition of shakuhachi making comparable to Japan's.

fashion.) The key of D is also very useful, especially for traditional folk music.

Only six finger holes are necessary to play the full eight-note scale, plus nearly all the sharps and flats, in two octaves. (A thumb hole is not necessary on the flute, as it is on the recorder, since the second octave is produced completely by lip adjustment.) Some folk flutes, however, have as many as nine finger holes. These can make the sharps and flats come out a little better; on the other hand, playing these flutes is a little more complicated, and the extra holes may make it harder to hold the flute steady. Whether the advantages outweigh the disadvantages is a matter of personal preference.

Make sure that you can reach and completely

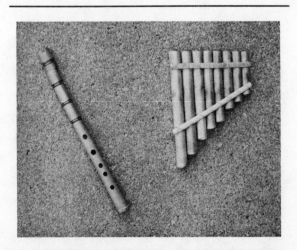

Figure 102

note of the second octave with all fingers on. The flute should play a full two octaves. Further marks of quality include: thick bamboo; an inlaid blowing edge; a lacquered interior; separation into two joints; and relatively easy blowing.

Other End-Blown Flutes

Kena. This was originally the name of the traditional Andean instrument (see chapter 1), but today it is applied by folk flute makers to any end-blown flute with a notched blowing edge. Most of these are tuned in a regular Western scale, and they can be evaluated in much the same way as a side-blown flute.

Panpipes and nay. These can occasionally be found, but they are not yet commonly produced by Western folk flute makers.

18
Caring for a Folk Flute

Bamboo

Though normally a very sturdy material, bamboo may crack or split if subjected to rapid moisture or temperature changes that affect the inside and outside surfaces differently. While a crack confined to the surface will not affect the playing, any crack that reaches the interior will make the flute unplayable.

Here are some rules to follow: Shake out the moisture after playing, or better still, wipe it out. Keep the flute away from heaters and hot direct sunlight. Wrap it up when taking it out into the extreme cold. Never play when the flute is very cold.

Unless your flute is coated, it should be kept well oiled, inside and out, to repel moisture and to make the fibers less brittle. Use food or mineral oils only—commercial finishing oils, including "boiled" linseed oil, are toxic! Sesame and raw linseed oil (from a health food store) are good. At first, oil the flute daily—inside and out—until it stops soaking up the oil. After that, it will have to be oiled occasionally, because your saliva will draw the oil out of the wood.

Binding is extremely important in preventing serious cracks. If your flute is not already bound, or if the binding is loose, you can bind the flute yourself, as shown in figure 103. Any strong cord will do. Wrap it around a piece of dowel first, and unwind it from there onto the flute, pulling it tight as you go. Two binding places should be sufficient for the flute: between the mouth hole and the first finger hole, and at the bottom of the flute. These are the places at

1. MAKE A LOOP.

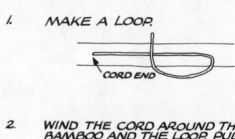
CORD END

2. WIND THE CORD AROUND THE BAMBOO AND THE LOOP. PULL EACH WINDING TIGHT!

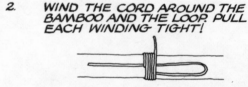

3. PULL TIGHTLY AT "A" UNTIL "B" IS TIGHT; ALSO, PULL CORD TIGHT HERE → AND CUT OFF.

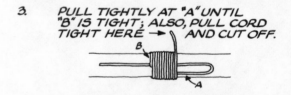
B
A

4. INSERT THE NEW END THRU THE LOOP, THEN PULL BOTH ENDS SO THAT...

5. THE LOOP IS PULLED UNDER THE WRAPPINGS, WHERE IT IS HELD BY FRICTION. CUT THE ENDS OFF FLUSH WITH THE WRAPPINGS.

Figure 103

which cracks are most likely to originate, though some flute makers prefer to bind the flute every couple of inches or so.

To repair a crack, cut the edges into a wedge shape, using a sharp razor blade or X-acto knife. Apply epoxy glue into the crack. (Excess epoxy can be wiped off with an alcohol-soaked rag.) When the glue has set, bind tightly along the crack. If the flute has actually split, the edges of the crack can be brought together and clamped by slipping a few loops of cord around the flute, and twisting them with a stick. You can also use motor hose bands, available from hardware and automotive stores. Be sure to bind the flute before removing the clamps.

Other Materials

Wood. Like bamboo, wood must be protected from moisture and temperature extremes to prevent cracking; it should be wiped dry after playing; and it should be kept well oiled, with food or mineral oil. (A special oil for wooden instruments is sold by music stores as *bore oil*.) If the flute cracks or splits, it can be brought to a regular musical instrument repair shop.

Ceramic. Ceramic flutes require no regular maintenance. When broken, they can be put back together with epoxy glue, porcelain cement, etc.

Metal and plastic. These require no maintenance or repair, though you may want to wash them occasionally in warm soapy water.

Corks

If your flute uses a cork to stop up the end, it has probably been placed in the best possible position; moving it may throw the flute out of tune and/or make it difficult to play. You

Figure 104

should know the exact placement of the cork, in case it gets moved accidentally. Measure this by inserting a stick into the flute until its end rests against the cork; then make a mark on the stick in the exact center of the portion that shows through the mouth hole (see figure 104).

If the cork has already been moved, and you need to relocate it, here's the procedure: Start with the cork about as close to the middle of the mouth hole as the length of the inside diameter of the flute. Shift the cork slightly forward and back, and test it in each position. To test, close all the holes for the left hand, and blow the note in the first octave, then in the second, without trying to "bend" either note into tune. When these two notes come closest to being in tune with each other, while still retaining their clarity of tone, the cork is in its optimal position. Another test is that, when the cork is properly placed, the two notes given by the fingering described above will normally be closer in tune than the two notes an octave apart of any other fingering.

Sometimes the original placement of the cork by the flute maker is not correct. To see if this is the case, use the second test given above. If you decide to experiment with moving the cork, first make a careful note of the original position—so you can change your mind if you want to! Then follow the procedure described above.

If a cork becomes loose, it can be coated with tallow, beeswax, or cork grease (available from music stores). Or a new one can be made, by taking any piece of cork, shaving it down with a sharp razor, and sanding it. It is essential that the cork be *absolutely airtight* for the flute to work properly.

19

Playing a Folk Flute*

Side-Blown Flutes

Getting a sound. Leave your fingers *off* the holes at first. Rest your bottom lip on the edge of the mouth hole, and blow it like a pop bottle (see figure 105).

Figure 105

Make sure the mouth hole is pointed directly upward, and that your head is held straight up. Your bottom lip must be resting *loosely* on the edge—not pulled up, or curled under itself, or pressed down hard against the flute. (On a wooden flute, you might want to press down a little harder than on other types.) Press your lips together at the corners, leaving a narrow opening at the front, centered above the mouth hole. Your top lip should slightly overhang the lower, and be about a third of an inch above the hole. Blow a solid stream of air directly at the opposite edge of the hole. Don't lift up your bottom lip as you blow.

If no sound comes, check your bottom lip to make sure you're not unconsciously pulling it up. Then rotate the flute to change the angle at

This chapter gives complete playing instructions for the folk flute beginner. However, for a more detailed discussion of some of the principles presented here, it is a good idea to read parts III and IV of this book.

which your breath hits the edge. Also, try varying the shape and pressure of your blowing. Looking in a mirror helps a great deal. If your lips get tired, it is best to take a break. Don't worry if you experience dizzy feelings—you just aren't used to breathing so deeply.

Practice the sound with your fingers off the holes until you can get it regularly.

Hand and body position. Hand position may vary on some flutes, according to the placement of the holes. Try to stick as closely as possible to the following description.

Hold the flute pointed toward the right, and place your hands on it as shown in figure 106. Notice that the left hand comes in at an angle, not straight on. On most six-hole flutes, the first three fingers (index, middle, and ring) of each hand are used to cover the holes. Sometimes the last hole will be covered more comfortably by the little finger instead. Some flutes have thumb holes, and/or additional holes to be covered by the remaining fingers.

Generally, the flute is supported at the following three points: (1) the *side* of the left index finger, which is curled *under* the flute to create a supporting cradle (see figure 106); (2) the right thumb, positioned directly under the right forefinger; and (3) either the ring or little finger of the right hand—whichever has no hole to cover—which is kept down on the flute *at all times*. If there is no thumb hole, the left thumb is used as an additional support; it is placed against the *side* of the flute, between the first and second holes (*not* pointed toward the mouth hole), as shown in figure 107. Never use

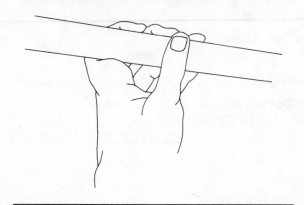

Figure 106

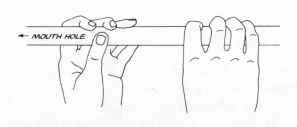

MOUTH HOLE →

Figure 107

Figure 108

your bottom lip to support the flute.

This hand position holds the flute so that it is absolutely steady—even when all fingers are off the holes—and you can play with full speed and facility.

Hold your body straight, with your elbows and shoulders kept down. Tilt the flute *slightly* down and forward. Your head is rotated to the left and tilted to the right—never bent forward—so that it's perpendicular to the flute (see figure 108). This posture will require the least muscle effort, while allowing you the fullest use and control of your breath.

Playing the notes. When you get the proper position, take all your fingers off the flute except those directly supporting it. With all the holes uncovered, blow a note, and while you're doing it cover the first hole (the one nearest the mouth hole). Cover it with the fleshy face of your finger, not the extreme tip. The hole must be covered so as to be completely airtight,

but the finger should not have to be pressed down too hard.

When you can get a good sound with the first hole covered, keep that finger down, and close the next hole in the same way, and so on, as long as the sound holds out. (Don't forget the thumb hole, if there is one.) Each note should be lower. As you go down the scale, your top lip should come slightly forward and down, and your lip opening should become larger and more relaxed.

If you lose the sound, start over from the top. Make sure each hole is completely covered. Keep doing this until you can get a good sound with all the holes covered. This series of notes is called the *first octave*.

Once you can play the first octave, you're ready to try the second. Cover all the holes, but narrow your lip opening and blow a little harder. The note you get will be much higher— the beginning of the second octave. To get the rest of the octave, take your fingers *off* the holes one at a time, starting with the bottom hole. Each note will be higher. Your upper lip should move gradually up and back, and your lip opening should become narrower and tighter, so that a stronger blowing pressure is needed to force the air out. Many flutes will allow you to reach the note with all holes open and then one

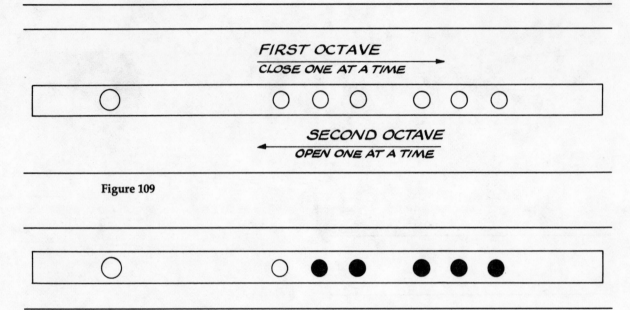

Figure 109

Figure 110

more note up, played with all the holes covered again.

There is a slight fingering irregularity on most flutes: The two higher notes that are played with all holes covered usually will have better tuning if you play them with the top hole open, as shown in figure 110.

On a six-hole flute, the fingerings you have just used will give you the main scale of the flute (repeated in each octave). In addition, you will probably be able to get most of the sharps and flats. (These are the notes between the notes. The sharp of a note is higher, the flat is lower.) One way to get them is to cover only half of the last hole fingered—this is called *half-holing*. A second way—called *cross-* or *fork-fingering*—is to skip that hole and close one or more of the holes below it. (See figure 111.) Experiment on

your flute to see how these methods work for particular notes.

When a flute has more than six holes, the extra holes are used to get particular sharps and flats. To find the main scale of one of these flutes, start with the lowest note (all fingers on), and lift your fingers from the bottom of the flute, one or two at a time, to play the notes of the do–re–mi scale. (These flutes often come with fingering charts.)

HALF-HOLING

CROSS-FINGERING

Figure 111

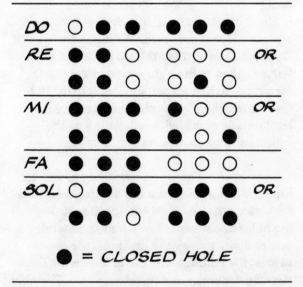

Figure 112

On some flutes you will be able to play into the third octave. The chart in figure 112 shows possible fingerings for the first half of that octave.

Other instructions. Always breathe from your stomach. On single notes, or the first note of a run-together series, start the note by making a light "t" sound with your tongue. Practice holding individual notes as long and as steadily as you can. When you have a fairly solid sound, you're ready to develop vibrato, a pulsing sound. To get it, pull in your stomach in short jerks, as in a belly laugh. Vibrato is used where you think it will sound good, and especially on long notes.

If your flute is tuned to a regular scale, you will be able to play most songs on it. You will also be able to play written music—either by finding out what notes your flute plays, or by "assigning" a particular written note to the low note of the flute. I personally recommend learning to play by ear, however. Choose simple melodies and pick out the notes on the flute. Find the note to start on that will give you as few sharps and flats in the song as possible.

You can tune the flute slightly, to play with others, by rotating it forward or back, but the tone and tuning are always best when you use the proper angle.

Shakuhachi

These instructions are for Japanese-style shakuhachi, but they can be easily adapted to other kinds of shakuhachi as well.

Rest the mouth hole end on your upper chin, holding the flute pointing down and away at about a 45-degree angle, with the main finger holes facing up. Leave your fingers off the holes for now. Lay your bottom lip over the open end, so that it covers nearly all of it, but not the curved blowing edge. Keep your head up and stick your jaw forward slightly. Blow steadily, directly at the blowing edge, as if into a pop bottle (see figure 114). Don't raise your bottom lip! If you have trouble, try moving your jaw forward and back as you blow, or change the

Figure 113

Figure 114

angle of the flute. Blowing the shakuhachi will become much easier with a little practice.

The flute is held and fingered as shown in figure 115. (Right and left hands can be switched, if you like.) It is held steady by the middle fingers of each hand, the right thumb, and your chin, all of which are in contact with the flute at all times.

Go up and down the notes of the flute in the same way as described for the side-blown flute earlier in this chapter. On many shakuhachi, the fifth note in the second octave will need a slightly irregular fingering, as shown in figure 116. Also, to get the first note of the third octave, you may have to open the back hole just a sliver.

The Japanese style of playing incorporates many devices almost unknown in the West. One of the most common consists of tilting the head forward and back to cover more or less of the open end—"nodding and bobbing," as one flute maker calls it—which changes the pitch of the note. This is used in addition to half-holing and cross-fingering (see the discussion in the

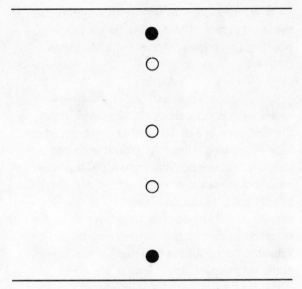

Figure 116

previous section on playing side-blown flutes) to produce notes other than the five main notes. Another use is to create note *slides*. Vibrato is also produced by this bobbing, rather than by diaphragm movements, as in the West.

If you would like to play the shakuhachi in an authentic Japanese style, the best way by far to learn is to locate a teacher. If this is not possible, two excellent introductory manuals are listed at the end of this book. But without going to all that trouble, you'll find that you can play any of the regular notes in any order, and get a lovely, haunting melody. There are no "wrong notes" in a pentatonic scale!

Other End-Blown Flutes

Kena. The instructions for getting a sound on the kena are basically the same as for the shakuhachi, while the fingering and playing of notes are similar to those of the side-blown flute. In the Andes, the kena is usually played with a throat vibrato, created by a rapid fluctuation of the throat muscles.

Panpipes. These are played exactly like pop bottles.

Nay. Hints on playing the nay are given in chapter 1.

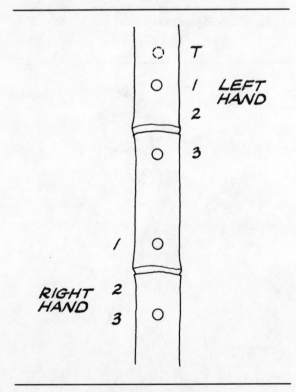

Figure 115

Appendix

how the Flute Works

A Tube with Holes

Nearly all musical instruments are made up of two basic elements: a generator, which gets the vibration going, and a resonator, which amplifies the vibration and modifies it to create the sound of the instrument.

On the flute, the generator is the mouth hole edge against which the player's breath is directed. When the breath meets the edge, it

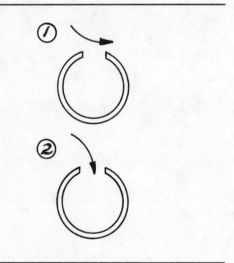

Figure 118

does not, as might be expected, divide into two separate air streams. Instead, the air stream rapidly fluctuates between going all into the hole and going all away from the hole. This sets up a rapid vibration at the head of the tube.

The remainder of the flute tube is the resonator—or more accurately, the container for the resonator, the actual resonator being the air within the tube. (The mechanisms on the outside of the flute are for the sole purpose of opening and closing the holes, and they have nothing to do with creating the sound.) Acoustically speaking, this tube is considered to be open at both ends, since the mouth hole acts as if it were an open end. So if we close all the note holes, the resonator-tube can be seen as figure 119.

Because the tube walls constrict air inside, that air acts like a stiff spring, fairly independent of the air surrounding it. When the air stream at the mouth hole begins fluctuating in and out of the tube, this air-spring receives a rapid succession of tiny pushes, and begins vibrating.

It does *not*, however, vibrate at the same rate as the vibration at the mouth hole. Since that vibration is so weak, it allows the air-spring to use the energy it's receiving to start vibrating in

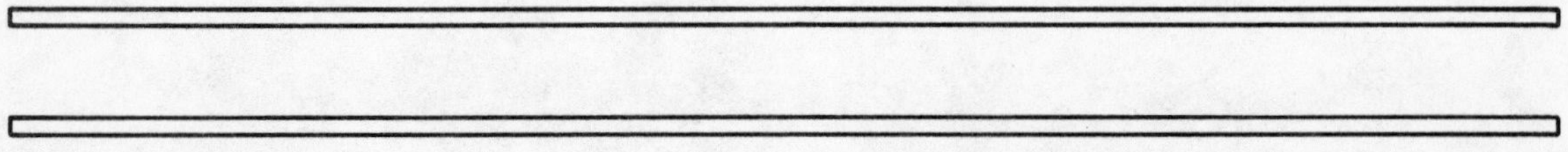

Figure 119

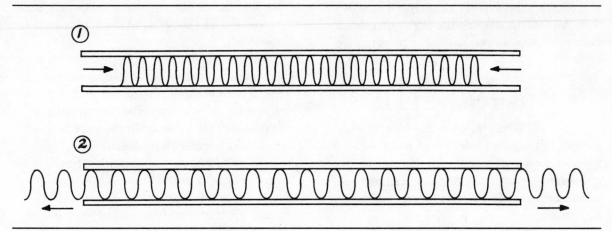

Figure 120

its own natural rhythm. This natural rhythm is determined by the length of the air-spring. When this vibration is set up, the movement of the air in the tube becomes a series of contractions and expansions that looks something like figure 120.

Because of the constricted nature of the air-spring, it retains a portion of the energy imparted to it and thereby grows in strength. It soon overpowers the weak fluctuations at the mouth hole and makes their timing conform to its own rhythm. When this happens, the pushes given by the mouth hole fluctuations occur simultaneously with each contraction of the air-spring. This is something like a person pushing a swing. It makes the vibration build up to a point at which it can vibrate the air around it, vibrate the air around it, and a note is heard.

This note can be altered very slightly by breath and lip adjustments, but to change it completely (short of changing octaves), the

length of the air-spring itself must be changed. This is done by opening a hole in the side of the tube. The hole removes the constriction of the air at that point—it's almost as if the tube were cut off there. Now the air-spring only goes as far as that open hole (see figure 121). If another hole is opened closer to the mouth hole, the air-spring will end there instead. The vibrating portion of the tube will aways be (at least on the first octave) between the mouth hole and the first open hole beneath it.

The shorter the air-spring, the faster its natural rhythm and the higher the note it will produce. To go up the first octave of the flute, then, the flutist opens one hole at a time from the bottom, shortening the air-spring a little with each hole opened.

To get an idea of the dimensions we're talking about, on a modern flute with all holes closed, the air-spring will contract and expand 262 times per second; with all the holes opened, it

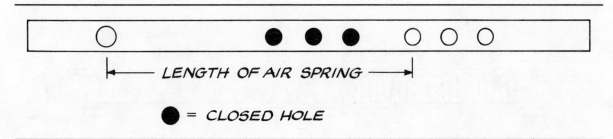

Figure 121

will contract and expand a little more than twice that. An individual molecule of air will move in either direction an average of one hundredth of an inch!

Harmonics

While the air in the flute tube is moving in the pattern described above—called the *fundamental* vibration—it's also moving in a number of *harmonic* vibrations. These are additional natural patterns of vibration for the air-spring.

As an example, let's close up the holes in the tube again and take a look at the first harmonic. In this pattern of vibration, the air-spring acts as if it were divided into two equal sections. Just as the entire air-spring does in the fundamental vibration, each half alternately contracts and expands, but in opposite timing to each other, so that one is contracting while the other is expanding. It looks something like figure 122. Each section, being half the length of the original air-spring, vibrates at a rate twice as fast as the fundamental vibration.

The air in the tube is also moving in a *second* harmonic vibration, in which the air-spring is divided into *three* sections; in a *third* harmonic vibration, dividing the air-spring into *four* sections; and so on, up to the sixth harmonic— even higher for some fingerings. All these ways of vibrating are occurring in the flute tube *at the same time.* And if we open holes in the tube, all

these vibrational patterns will then be occurring between the mouth hole and the first open hole beneath it.

How is it possible for all these vibrations to be happening simultaneously? To understand this it might help to think of these vibrations not so much as actual movements of the air, but as the movement of *forces that act on* the air. If an individual air molecule inside the tube were pushed by two opposing vibrational forces at the same time, it would move in the direction of the stronger; if they were equal, it wouldn't move at all. If the two forces were going in the same direction, it would move in that direction an extra amount.

You may have seen something like this if you've ever played with a long rope attached at one end. You can send a vibration down the rope, then another one shortly after. The first vibration will bounce back at the other end, and when the two vibrations meet, they will pass through each other.

Let's return to the first harmonic. We said before that the two equal sections were each vibrating at a rate double that of the fundamental. This produces a separate *harmonic note,* one octave higher than the *fundamental note.* Each additional harmonic vibration also creates its own harmonic note, and these are all going on at the same time as the fundamental.

These notes, however, are so closely related that they blend together, and we hear them as one note, rather than separately. Yet they make

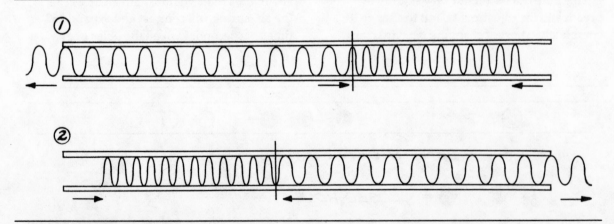

Figure 122

a big difference in the *tone*. On any instrument, tone is determined by the relative strength of the harmonics. The *nature* of the vibrations of all instrument sounds is identical—for instance, the fundamental vibration of the note C is the same whether it is played by a flute, a violin, or a tuning fork. What creates the differences in sounds is the *combination* of the vibrations. This is something like creating many different recipes from a given set of ingredients, by varying selection and amounts. The flute sound has fewer types of harmonic vibration than almost any other instrument, and this is the main factor in the production of its distinctive tone.

Octaves

Harmonics are also important in the production of the higher octaves.

When the ear hears a fundamental and various harmonics all together, it interprets the lowest note—in this case the fundamental—as "the" note, and hears the rest as tone. To produce the flute's second octave, then, we have to *take out* the fundamental, so that the first harmonic—which is one octave higher—will be the lowest note heard.

This is done through lip and breath adjustment. By a combination of speeding up your breath and pushing your lips closer to the mouth hole edge, you cut in half the "travel time" of the air stream. At this point the fluctuations of the air stream "double-time" and hook up with the first harmonic. The fundamental, left without support, drops out, leaving the first harmonic as the lowest note, and causing the second octave to be heard. This is why the second octave can be produced using the same fingerings as the first.

If the travel time of the air stream is cut down still further, the air stream fluctuations will hook into the third and then the fourth harmonics, dropping the previous, slower harmonic at each step. Both the third and the fourth harmonics are used in the production of the third octave.

To make the notes of the third octave easier to play, *venting* is also used. (On the second octave, venting is used on the D and D-sharp.) In venting, you open a hole somewhere along the vibrating portion of the tube, thereby removing the constriction at that point and introducing a "weak spot" into the air-spring. This forcibly divides the air-spring, guaranteeing that the lower harmonic will have to drop out. (In the higher octaves, more than a single note hole has to be opened to completely divide the air-spring.) Venting also improves the tuning on some notes.

This is only a brief, partial account of what is known about the complexities of sound production in the flute. Furthermore, scientists still have far to go in unraveling the mysteries of this simple tube with holes.

Miscellaneous Fingering Charts

The following charts show fingerings for different types of flutes that you may encounter. The first two (figures 123 and 124) are taken from *A Treatise on the Construction, the History, and the Practice of the Flute,* by R. S. Rockstro (1890). The third (figure 125) is from *The Flute and Flute-Playing,* by Theobald Boehm (1871). (Notice that in the diagram accompanying figure 125 the placement of the thumb key and the B-flat key is the reverse of that found in current flute construction. This does not, however, affect the chart.)

Figure 123